Dandelion

Recipes

© Copyright 2018. Laura Sommers.
All rights reserved.
No part of this book may be reproduced in any form or by any electronic or mechanical means without written permission of the author. All text, illustrations and design are the exclusive property of
Laura Sommers

Introduction 1
Appalachian Fried Dandelions 2
Dandelion Greens... 3
Dandelion Pumpkin Seed Pesto 4
Linguine with Mussels and Dandelion Greens.......... 5
Dandelion Jelly 6
Dandelion Greens with Garlic and Almonds 7
Dandelion Salad with Tomato Dressing..................... 8
Dandelion Greens with Roasted Garlic Dressing..... 9
Dandelion Mexican Meatball Soup (Albondigas) ...10
Thai Red Curry with Dandelion Greens.................... 11
Sautéed Mushroom Dandelion Salad........................ 12
Dandelion Quesadillas... 13
Dandelion Greens with Toasted Mustard Seed 14
Dandelion Wine 15
Dandelion Syrup.. 16
Dandelion Root Tea.. 16
Dandelion Root Coffee... 17
Warm Dandelion Greens and Bacon 17
Dandelion Dressing... 18
Deep-Fried Dandelions 19
Dandelion and Tomato Salad Appetizer.................... 20

Lavender Dandelion Cookies	21
Dandelion Soup	22
Creamy Dandelion Soup	23
Dandelion Stew	24
Dandelion Potatoes	25
Chinese Dandelion Dumplings	26
Dandelion Flower Cookies	27
Dandelion Greens and Tortellini Soup	28
Sautéed Dandelion Greens	29
Dandelion Bread	30
Tuna Salad with Dandelion	31
Sautéed Dandelions and Pine Nuts	31
Dandelion Slaw	32
Dandelion with Kiwi	33
Mediterranean Dandelion Greens	33
Orzo with Dandelion Greens	34
Dandelion Cheese Crisps	35
Dandelion and Feta Salad	35
Spinach and Dandelion Smoothie	36
Tropical Dandelion Smoothie	36
Dandelion and Quinoa Salad	37
Waldorf Dandelion Salad	38
Dandelion Yam Wrap	38
Creamy Parmesan Dandelion Chicken	39

Dandelion Sweet Potato Bake 40

Dandelion Root "Carrots" 41

Red Potato and Sautéed Greens Salad 41

Spicy Sautéed Dandelion Greens and Onions 42

Dandelion Greens with Eggs 43

Pasta with Sausage and Dandelion Greens 43

Dandelion Fritters 44

Dandelion Salad with Honey Dressing 45

Breaded Dandelion Blossoms 46

Wilted Bacon Dandelions 46

Scalloped Dandelions 47

Dandelion and Lime Iced Tea 47

Pennsylvania Dutch Dandelion Salad 48

Italian Sausage and Dandelions 49

Pan-Fried Beans and Dandelion Greens 49

Lemon and Garlic Sautéed Dandelions 50

Dandelion Vinegar 51

Brown Rice and Dandelion Salad 51

Boiled Dandelion Greens 52

Dandelion Greens Salad 53

Cauliflower Dandelion Soup 53

Dandelion Burgers 54

Korean Cauliflower Dandelion Pancakes 54

Dandelion Moonshine 55

Dandelion Flower Tea	56
Dandelion and Lemon Biscuits	56
Dandelion Flower Pasta	57
Dandelion Mead	58
Dandelion Greens Sauté	60
Dandelion Frittata	61
Mushroom Garlic Dandelion Quiche	62
Dandelion Tart	63
Dandelion Leek Frittata	64
Dandelion Lemon Cupcakes	65
Dandelion Sun Dried Tomato Bake	66
Dandelion Root Zucchini Cake	67
Rhubarb Dandelion Pie	68
Dandelion Root Bitters	69
Dandelion Squash Salad with Quinoa	69
Blueberry Dandelion Green Smoothie	70
Dandelion Peanut Butter Cookies	71
Dandelion Honey	72
Dandelion Petal Sorbet	73
Dandelion Flower Schnapps	73
Dandelion Root Schnapps	74
Dandelion Petal Risotto	75
Dandelion Lip Balm	76
Dandelion Jam	76

Dandelion Curried Red Lentil Soup 77
Dandelion Tacos 78
Dandelion Zucchini Muffins 79
Tuscan Dandelion and Cannellini Bean Soup 80
Dandelion Pasta 81
Dandelion Cabbage Soup 81
Stuffed Dandelion Leaves 82
Dandelion Cannelloni 83
Dandelion Bisque 84
Dandelion Almond Loaf 85
Raisin and Pine Nuts Dandelion Fettuccine 86
Dandelion Patties 87
Dandelion Minestrone Soup 88
About the Author 89
Other Cookbooks by Laura Sommers 90

Introduction

For many, harvesting wild dandelion is a beloved springtime ritual. Learn how to use dandelions and enjoy the health benefits of dandelion greens in a variety of ways.

All parts of the dandelion can be foraged and used in different ways, from the roots to the leaves to the flowers. If you have the proper recipes and know how to prepare them, dandelions can be a tasty wonderful treat. And the best thing is that they are free!

Appalachian Fried Dandelions

Ingredients:

2 cups all-purpose flour
2 tbsps. seasoned salt
1 tbsp. ground black pepper
4 eggs
80 unopened dandelion blossoms, stems removed
1/2 cup butter

Directions:

1. Combine the flour, seasoned salt, and pepper in a mixing bowl until evenly combined; set aside. Beat the eggs in a mixing bowl, then stir in the dandelion blossoms until completely coated.
2. Melt the butter in a large skillet over medium heat.
3. Remove half of the dandelions from the egg, and allow the excess egg to drip away.
4. Toss in the flour until completely coated, then remove from the flour, tossing between your hands to allow excess flour to fall away.
5. Cook the dandelions in the melted butter until golden brown, stirring occasionally, about 5 minutes.
6. Drain on a paper towel-lined plate.
7. Repeat with the remaining dandelions.

Dandelion Greens

Ingredients:

1 pound dandelion greens, torn into 4-inch pieces
1 tsp. salt
2 tbsps. olive oil
1 tbsp. butter
1/2 onion, thinly sliced
1/4 tsp. red pepper flakes
2 cloves garlic, minced
Salt and ground black pepper to taste
1 tbsp. grated Parmesan cheese (optional)

Directions:

1. Soak dandelion greens in a large bowl of cold water with 1 tsp. salt for 10 minutes.
2. Drain.
3. Bring a large pot of water to a boil with 1 tsp. salt.
4. Cook greens until tender, 3 to 4 minutes.
5. Drain and rinse with cold water until chilled.
6. Heat olive oil and butter in a large skillet over medium heat; cook and stir onion and red pepper flakes until onion is tender, about 5 minutes.
7. Stir in garlic until garlic is fragrant, about 30 seconds more. Increase heat to medium-high and add dandelion greens.
8. Continue to cook and stir until liquid is evaporated, 3 to 4 minutes.
9. Season with salt and black pepper.
10. Sprinkle greens with Parmesan cheese to serve.

Dandelion Pumpkin Seed Pesto

Ingredients:

3/4 cup unsalted hulled (green) pumpkin seeds
3 garlic gloves, minced
1/4 cup freshly grated parmesan
1 bunch dandelion greens (about 2 cups, loosely packed)
1 tbsp. lemon juice
1/2 cup extra-virgin olive oil
1/2 tsp. kosher salt
Black pepper, to taste

Directions:

1. Preheat the oven to 350 degrees F.
2. Pour the pumpkin seeds onto a shallow-rimmed baking sheet and roast until just fragrant, about 5 minutes.
3. Remove from the oven and allow to cool.
4. Pulse the garlic and pumpkin seeds together in the bowl of a food processor until very finely chopped.
5. Add parmesan cheese, dandelion greens, and lemon juice and process continuously until combined. Stop the processor every now and again to scrape down the sides of the bowl.
6. The pesto will be very thick and difficult to process after awhile which is ok.
7. With the blade running, slowly pour in the olive oil and process until the pesto is smooth.
8. Add salt and pepper to taste.

Linguine with Mussels and Dandelion Greens

Ingredients:

2 pounds mussels
1 pkg. (1 lb.) linguine
1 Tbsp. salt
1 Tbsp. olive oil
1/2 onion, minced
3 cloves garlic, minced
3 tbsps. sun-dried tomatoes, minced
1 tsp. red pepper flakes
1 cup of beer
1 bunch dandelion greens, cut cross-wise into thin ribbons
1 tbsp. lemon juice (about 1/2 lemon)
Salt and pepper to taste

Directions:

1. Clean all the mussels and de-beard by tugging off the brown 'tag' coming out of the side of the mussel.
2. Bring a large pot of water to a boil, add the salt, and cook the linguine according to the package.
3. Drain and set aside.
4. Meanwhile, heat the olive oil in a large wide-bottomed skillet or saucepan with a lid.
5. Add the onions and sauté until translucent--about 5 minutes.
6. Add the garlic, sun-dried tomatoes, and red pepper flakes, and sauté until fragrant--about 30 seconds.
7. Add the mussels to the pan, pour in the beer, and cover immediately with the lid.
8. Cook for about five minutes, shaking once or twice, until all the shells have opened.
9. Discard any unopened shells.
10. Add the dandelion greens to the pan and stir occasionally until the greens are wilted.
11. Add the linguine to the pan and toss with mussels and greens.
12. Season with the lemon juice, salt, and pepper.

Dandelion Jelly

Ingredients:

3 cups packed fresh dandelion blossoms
4 cups water
4 cups sugar
1 box powdered pectin
2 tbsps. lemon juice
1 drop yellow food coloring

Directions:

1. Using your thumb fingernail, cut and pluck the yellow blossom out of the tiny green leaves holding it. (Your thumb will get sticky and the flower will separate into petals.)
2. Remove as much of the green as possible because green is bitter and turns the jelly green.
3. By now, your blossoms will weigh about 2.35 oz.
4. In a medium saucepan, bring water to a boil.
5. Add half the blossoms, stir.
6. Cover.
7. Turn off water and steep for 20 minutes.
8. Using a fine mesh strainer, strain out and gently push on blossoms to remove some of the water.
9. Add the same dandelion water back to saucepan and bring to a boil.
10. Add remaining blossoms; cover. Steep 15 minutes.
11. Strain out blossoms, pressing to remove water.
12. Measure steeping liquid to 3 cups; add sugar, pectin, lemon juice and (optional) food coloring and bring to a boil, stirring until sugar dissolves.
13. Boil for 1 minute, then skim off foam with a wooden spoon.
14. Pour into hot sterilized half-pint jars leaving 1/4-inch headspace and store in the refrigerator or process according to canner manufacturer's instructions.

Dandelion Greens with Garlic and Almonds

Ingredients:

1 large bunch dandelion greens, trimmed and coarsely chopped
3 tbsps. extra-virgin olive oil
6 cloves garlic, thinly sliced
4 scallions, thinly sliced, whites and about 2 inches of the greens only
1/3 cup sliced blanched almonds, toasted
1/4 tsp. salt

Directions:

1. Bring a large pot of water to a boil.
2. Drop greens into the boiling water and cook until bright green, stirring once or twice, 30 seconds to 2 minutes, depending on the type of greens.
3. Drain in a colander, then rinse well with cold water.
4. Drain again, pressing on the greens to remove excess water.
5. Heat oil in a large skillet over medium-high heat.
6. Add garlic and scallions; cook, stirring, until the garlic starts to turn golden brown, 30 seconds to 2 minutes.
7. Add the greens and cook, stirring, until tender and heated through, 1 to 3 minutes.
8. Stir in almonds and season with salt.
9. Serve and enjoy!

Dandelion Salad with Tomato Dressing

Dressing Ingredients:

1/4 cup crumbled goat cheese
2 tbsps. white wine vinegar
2 tsps. maple syrup
1/4 cup extra-virgin olive oil
2 plum tomatoes, seeded and chopped
1/2 tsp. salt
Freshly ground pepper, to taste
1 tbsp. chopped fresh tarragon
8 oz. orecchiette, or small pasta shells
2 slices bacon
1 tbsp. extra-virgin olive oil
1 medium red onion, thinly sliced
2 cups chopped dandelion greens
2 cups baby spinach
1/4 cup grated Parmesan cheese

Dressing Directions:

1. Combine goat cheese, vinegar and maple syrup in a blender or food processor and blend until combined.
2. Add 1/4 cup oil and tomatoes and blend until smooth.
3. Season with salt and pepper.
4. Stir in tarragon.

Salad Directions:

1. Bring a large saucepan of water to a boil.
2. Add pasta and cook according to package directions.
3. Drain, rinse with cold water and set aside.
4. Cook bacon in a large skillet over medium heat until crisp, about 4 minutes.
5. Drain on a paper towel.
6. Crumble when cool. Wipe out the pan.
7. Add 1 tbsp. oil and onion and cook, stirring, over medium heat until soft, about 5 minutes. Let cool.

8. When the bacon and onion are cool, toss them in a large bowl with dandelion greens, spinach, Parmesan and 1/2 cup dressing.
9. Drizzle more dressing over each serving, if desired.

Dandelion Greens with Roasted Garlic Dressing

Ingredients:

Roasted garlic dressing
1 large head garlic, roasted
3 tbsps. extra-virgin olive oil
2 tbsps. balsamic vinegar or red-wine vinegar
1 tbsp. lime juice
1/8 tsp. salt
1 medium shallot, finely chopped
Freshly ground pepper to taste
1/4 cup pine nuts, toasted
2 oz. goat cheese, crumbled
6 cups dandelion greens, chopped

Directions:

1. Squeeze roasted garlic pulp into a blender or food processor and discard the skins.
2. Add oil, vinegar, lime juice, salt and pepper and blend or process until smooth.
3. Transfer the dressing to a small saucepan and place over medium heat until warm, 1 to 2 minutes.
4. Add shallot and simmer until the shallot is softened, 3 to 5 minutes.
5. Place dandelion greens in a large salad bowl.
6. Pour the warm dressing over the greens and toss until they are wilted and coated.
7. Add pine nuts and goat cheese and toss again, slightly melting the cheese with the warm greens.
8. Season with pepper.
9. Serve and enjoy!

Dandelion Mexican Meatball Soup (Albondigas)

Ingredients:

4 cups chicken or beef broth
4 cups water
1-2 limes, divided
4 oz. fresh chorizo, casing removed (1-2 links)
1/2 cup fine whole-grain cornmeal
1/2 cup finely chopped scallions
1/2 cup finely chopped fresh cilantro
1 large egg
2 cloves garlic, minced
1 tsp. dried oregano
1/4 tsp. freshly ground pepper
1 1/4 pounds lean ground beef
6 cups chopped dandelion greens
1 cup sliced carrots
1-2 chipotle chiles in adobo sauce, minced
1 cup corn kernels, fresh or frozen

Directions:

1. Bring broth and water to a simmer in a Dutch oven over medium heat.
2. Meanwhile, zest and juice 1 lime; reserve the juice.
3. Break up chorizo in a large bowl.
4. Mix in cornmeal, scallions, cilantro, egg, garlic, oregano, pepper and the lime zest.
5. Add meat. Gently mix to combine (do not overmix).
6. Using 1 tbsp. for each, make about 40 small meatballs.
7. Add dandelion greens, carrots and chipotle to taste to the simmering broth mixture, then add the meatballs.
8. Simmer until the meatballs are cooked through and the vegetables are tender, 10 to 12 minutes.
9. Stir in corn and cook until heated through, 1 to 2 minutes more.
10. Stir in 2 tbsps. lime juice.
11. Serve with lime wedges and enjoy!

Thai Red Curry with Dandelion Greens

Ingredients:

1 14-oz. can coconut milk, divided
2 tbsps. Thai red curry paste, or to taste
1 lb. sweet potatoes, peeled and cut into 1 1/2-inch cubes
2 cups water
1 bunch asparagus, trimmed and cut into 2-inch lengths
2 fresh cayenne chiles or bird chiles, cut into long strips
2 whole lime leaves
2 tsps. lime zest
2 cups coarsely chopped dandelion greens
1/2 cup fresh basil leaves, preferably Thai basil
1/4 tsp. salt

Directions:

1. Heat a wide heavy pot over medium-high heat.
2. Add about 2 tbsps. coconut milk and curry paste, stirring to dissolve it.
3. Cook, stirring, until aromatic, 30 seconds to 1 minute.
4. Add 1 cup of the coconut milk and cook for 1 minute, then add sweet potatoes.
5. Stir to coat the pieces and cook, stirring frequently, for 3 minutes more.
6. Add water and bring to a boil.
7. Cook until the sweet potatoes are almost cooked through, about 5 minutes.
8. Add the remaining coconut milk, asparagus, chiles (if using) and lime leaves (or lime zest); cook for 1 minute.
9. Stir in dandelion greens (or arugula), basil and salt until well combined.
10. Continue cooking until the asparagus is just tender, 1 to 2 minutes more.
11. Remove lime leaves, if necessary, before serving.
12. Red curry paste is a blend of chile peppers, garlic, lemongrass and galangal (a root with a flavor similar to ginger).
13. Look for it in jars or cans in the Asian section of the supermarket or specialty stores.

14. The heat and salt level can vary widely depending on brand.
15. Be sure to taste as you go.
16. Serve and enjoy!

Sautéed Mushroom Dandelion Salad

Ingredients:

2 tbsps. extra-virgin olive oil, divided
1 small onion, halved and sliced
1 lb. white or cremini mushrooms, quartered
2 cloves garlic, minced
1 1/2 tsps. chopped fresh thyme, or 1/2 tsp. dried
3 tbsps. dry sherry
2 tbsps. lemon juice
1/4 tsp. salt
1/4 tsp. freshly ground pepper
8 cups dandelion greens
2 tbsps. grated Parmesan cheese

Directions:

1. Heat 1 tbsp. oil in a large nonstick skillet over medium heat.
2. Add onion and cook until softened, about 3 minutes.
3. Add mushrooms and cook, stirring, until they release their juices, 10 to 12 minutes.
4. Add garlic and thyme and stir until fragrant, about 30 seconds.
5. Add sherry and cook until mostly evaporated, about 3 minutes.
6. Stir in the remaining 1 tbsp. oil, lemon juice, salt and pepper and continue cooking for 1 minute more.
7. Pour over greens in a large bowl and toss to coat.
8. Sprinkle with Parmesan.
9. Serve and enjoy!

Dandelion Quesadillas

Ingredients:

4 cups dandelion greens, roughly chopped
1/2 of a medium onion, finely chopped
1 garlic clove, minced
3 tbsps. butter or coconut oil
1 medium tomato, finely chopped
4 oz cream cheese, softened (how to make cream cheese)
1 1/2 cups shredded cheese
Sea salt and black pepper to taste
Flour tortillas

Directions:

1. In a medium frying pan, sauté the onion in the butter until the onion is soft and translucent.
2. Add the minced garlic and cook for 1-2 minutes more.
3. Add the dandelion greens to the pan and allow them to wilt for 3-4 minutes.
4. It will look like a massive quantity at first, but will quickly reduce in size.
5. Place the cream cheese, tomato, and shredded cheese in a separate bowl.
6. Mix in the spinach/onion mixture.
7. Season with salt & pepper as needed.
8. Spread two to four tbsps. of the mixture on half of each tortilla. Fold the tortilla in half.
9. Heat the tortilla in a lightly greased pan, flipping once.
10. Your quesadillas are done when they are a lovely shade of golden brown on both sides and the cheese is melted.
11. Serve and enjoy!

Dandelion Greens with Toasted Mustard Seed

Ingredients:

1 tbsp. whole mustard seed
2 tsp. clarified butter/ghee
4 oz. bacon, (chopped)
1 small shallot, chopped
1 pound young dandelion greens, rinsed well and coarsely chopped
2 tsps. red wine vinegar

Directions:

1. Place a cast iron or stainless steel skillet over a high flame and toss in mustard seeds, toasting gently until they release their fragrance – about two minutes.
2. Transfer mustard seed to a bowl or dish to cool while you prepare the remaining ingredients.
3. Reduce the heat to medium and spoon one tsp. butter into the skillet, allowing it to melt until it begins to froth.
4. Add chopped bacon to the butter and fry it until crisped and its fat rendered.
5. Transfer the bacon to the dish holding your toasted mustard seed.
6. Toss chopped shallot into the rendered bacon fat and fry until fragrant and softened, about three minutes.
7. Stir in dandelion greens into the chopped shallot and bacon fat, and immediately turn off the heat as the greens will wilt in the skillet's residual heat.
8. Pour in two tsps. red wine vinegar and continue stirring the greens until wilted to your liking.
9. Serve and enjoy!

Dandelion Wine

Ingredients:

3 quarts dandelion blossoms
1 gallon water
2 oranges, with peel
1 lemon, with peel
3 lbs. sugar
1 pkg. wine yeast
1 lb. raisins

Directions:

1. Collect the blossoms when they are fully open on a sunny day.
2. Remove any green parts as they will impair fermentation and ruin the taste of the wine.
3. Bring the water to a boil and pour it over the flowers in a large pot or crock.
4. Cover and let steep for three days.
5. Prepare the oranges and the lemon by zesting about half the skin off and cut the rest off in very thin strips to minimize the amount of white pith.
6. Peel the citrus completely and slice into thin rounds.
7. Add the orange and lemon zest to the flower-water mixture and bring to a boil.
8. Remove from heat, strain out solids and add the sugar stirring until it is dissolve.
9. Allow to cool.
10. Add the orange and lemon slices, yeast, and raisins to the liquid.
11. Put everything into a crock with a loose lid (so gas can escape) to ferment.
12. Cover it with a clean cotton towel held down by a rubber band.
13. Stir daily with a wooden spoon or non-reactive stir stick.
14. When the mixture has stopped bubbling (1-2 weeks), fermentation is complete.
15. Strain the liquid through several layers of cheesecloth and transfer to sterilized bottles.
16. Slip a deflated balloon over the top of each bottle to monitor for further fermentation.

17. When the balloon remains deflated for 24 hours, fermentation is complete.
18. Cork the bottles and store in a cool, dark place for at least six months before drinking.

Dandelion Syrup

Ingredients:

125 dandelion flowers (about 1 1/2 cups of petals)
3 cups water
2 – 3 cups sugar
1/4 – 1/2 cup raw honey
Juice of half a lemon (optional)

Directions:

1. Wash flowers and dry on a towel. With a knife, cut off the petals as close to the base as possible.
1. Put petals in a medium pot and cover with water.
2. Bring to a rolling boil, and allow to boil for 30-60 seconds.
3. Remove from heat, cover, and allow to steep overnight in a cool place. A cool counter or the fridge is ideal.
4. Next morning, strain the liquid into a sieve over a bowl.
5. Use the back of a spoon to squeeze out and extract as much liquid as possible.
6. Return water to pot, add sugar and lemon, and simmer on low heat for 1-1 1/2 hours, stirring occasionally.
7. Check for desired consistency by dipping spoon into syrup, letting it cool a bit, then testing it with your finger.
8. Store in an airtight, glass container in the fridge.

Dandelion Root Tea

Ingredients:

Dried dandelion roots
Honey
Sugar
Milk or cream

Directions:

1. Coarsely chop the roots.
2. Set oven to 250 degrees F and insert the baking pan with the chopped dandelions for 2 to 3 hours until they are totally dry.
3. Make tea by treating it like any other loose leaf, and make it in your tea press, or with a tea infuser.
4. Add honey, sugar, milk, cream or anything else that you normally add to tea.
5. Serve and enjoy!

Dandelion Root Coffee

Ingredients:

1 tbsp. roasted dandelion root
2 tsp. of roasted carob
1 pinch of oatstraw
1 pinch of nettle leaf
1 pinch of stevia leaf, optional

Directions:

1. Combine herbs and steep for 10 minutes.
2. Strain and pour in to a coffee mug.
3. Add a nut or rice milk and a dab of coconut oil for sweetness.

Warm Dandelion Greens and Bacon

Ingredients:

3 slices bacon or Canadian bacon, diced
2 tsps. extra-virgin olive oil
1 clove garlic, minced
12 cups young dandelion greens, rinsed well and shaken dry
2 tbsps. balsamic or rice-wine vinegar
6 dandelion flowers

Directions:

1. Fry bacon in a large cast-iron skillet or Dutch oven over medium heat until edges curl, 2 to 3 minutes.

2. Remove from the pan and drain on paper towels.
3. Pour off excess fat from the pan and add oil.
4. Add garlic and cook, stirring occasionally, until light brown, 1 to 2 minutes.
5. Add still-damp greens, stir to coat them with the oil, cover pan and steam until just limp, about 3 minutes.
6. Add vinegar and the cooked bacon, toss lightly and serve.

Dandelion Dressing

Ingredients:

7 slices bacon
2 eggs, beaten
1/2 cup white sugar
1/2 tsp. salt
1 cup mayonnaise
1/3 cup apple cider vinegar
3 tbsps. all-purpose flour
1 1/2 cups milk
3/4 lb. torn dandelion greens

Directions:

1. Fry bacon in a large skillet set over medium heat until crisp.
2. Remove from the pan and drain on paper towels.
3. Reserve about 3 tbsps. of the drippings in the skillet.
4. In a medium bowl, whisk together the eggs, sugar, salt, mayonnaise, and cider vinegar. Set aside.
5. Heat the bacon grease in the skillet over medium heat. Whisk in the flour until smooth.
6. Cook, stirring constantly, until the flour is browned, about 10 minutes.
7. Gradually whisk in the milk so that no lumps form and bring to a boil while stirring constantly.
8. Pour a little hot milk into the egg mixture, whisking constantly.
9. Transfer egg mixture to the skillet.
10. Crumble the bacon into the skillet and add the dandelion greens.
11. Cook and stir just until the greens are wilted and heated through.

Deep-Fried Dandelions

Ingredients:

30 dandelion flowers
1 cup all-purpose flour
1 tsp. curry powder
1/2 tsp. salt
1 egg
1/2 cup lager-style beer, or more if needed
2 cups canola oil for frying

Directions:

1. Wash dandelions under cool running water and dry on paper towels.
2. Remove the green tendrils behind each flower.
3. Mix flour, curry powder, and salt together in a bowl or measuring cup.
4. Beat egg in a bowl; stir in flour mixture until smooth.
5. Add beer to mixture until batter is similar to runny pancake batter.
6. Add more beer if batter is too thick.
7. Heat oil in a small saucepan to 375 degrees F (190 degrees C).
8. If you don't have a thermometer, heat the oil until it begins to shimmer.
9. Dip dandelion flowers in the batter and gently drop in the hot oil, working in batches.
10. Fry flowers until golden, about 3 minutes.
11. Transfer cooked flowers to crumpled paper towels or on a wire rack; serve warm.

Dandelion and Tomato Salad Appetizer

Ingredients:

2 cups dandelion leaves
1 cup crumbled feta cheese
1/2 cup finely chopped onion
1/4 cup diced red bell pepper
1/4 cup diced yellow bell pepper
1 clove garlic, minced
1/2 cup red wine vinaigrette salad dressing
1 tsp. Worcestershire sauce
1/2 tsp. Italian seasoning
15 Roma tomatoes, halved and seeded
1/2 cup Parmesan cheese

Directions:

1. Cut dandelion leaf blades away from their mid-veins, which can be bitter.
2. Chop leaf blades.
3. Transfer to a large bowl; mix in feta cheese, onion, red bell pepper, yellow bell pepper, and garlic.
4. Stir salad dressing, Worcestershire sauce, and Italian seasoning into the bowl.
5. Cover with plastic wrap and chill until flavors combine, about 1 hour.
6. Stuff each tomato half with some of the dandelion mixture.
7. Sprinkle with Parmesan cheese.

Lavender Dandelion Cookies

Ingredients:

1/4 cup whole wheat flour
1/4 cup steel cut oats
2 tbsps. brown sugar
1 tbsp. flax seeds
1 tbsp. chia seeds
8 large dandelion blossoms, yellow petals only
1/8 tsp. dried lavender flowers
1 tsp. vanilla
3/4 cup water, or as needed

Directions:

1. Preheat oven to 350 degrees F (175 degrees C).
2. Lightly grease a baking sheet or line with parchment paper.
3. Combine flour, oats, brown sugar, flax, chia seeds, and dandelion petals in a bowl.
4. Crush lavender flowers with fingers; add to flour mixture.
5. Stir in vanilla extract and enough water to create a moist dough that holds together when squeezed.
6. Portion dough into 6 cookies and arrange on prepared baking sheet.
7. Bake in preheated oven until cookies are dry and fragrant, about 10 minutes.
8. Allow to cool before removing from baking sheet.

Dandelion Soup

Ingredients:

1 cup celery, diced
1 cup carrot, diced
1 cup onion, diced
4 tbsps. fresh basil, minced
2 tbsps. fresh oregano, minced
1 tbsp. cumin
4 tbsps. garlic, minced
1 tbsp. vegetable oil
4 cups dandelion greens, chopped
4 cups spinach, chopped
8 cups vegetable stock
1 bay leaf
1 cup corn kernel
2 cups white beans, cooked
1 cup potato, diced
1 tsp. salt
1 tsp. black pepper

Directions:

1. Sauté the celery, carrot, onion, basil, oregano, cumin and garlic in the vegetable oil until tender.
2. Add the stock, bay leaf, corn, beans and potatoes and simmer until the potatoes are tender.
3. Season with salt and pepper.
4. Serve and enjoy!

Creamy Dandelion Soup

Ingredients:

1 lb. dandelion greens, trimmed
1 tbsp. canola oil
1 tbsp. unsalted butter
1/2 cup finely chopped onion
1/4 cup all-purpose flour
2 cups chicken broth
1 1/2 cups fat-free milk
1/2 cup half-and-half
1/2 tsp. kosher salt
1/4 tsp. freshly ground black pepper
Sour cream (optional)
8 lemon wedges

Directions:

1. Separate 1 dandelion leaf from the bunch; thinly slice, and set aside.
2. Fill a large Dutch oven half full with water; bring to a boil.
3. Add remaining greens to boiling water; cover and cook for 2 minutes.
4. Drain.
5. Place greens in a food processor; process 30 seconds or until smooth.
6. Place oil and butter in a 3-quart saucepan.
7. Cook over medium heat until butter melts.
8. Add onion; sauté 3 minutes or until tender.
9. Sprinkle flour over onion mixture, stirring to coat.
10. Add broth and next 4 ingredients (through pepper), stirring with a whisk.
11. Stir in pureed greens.
12. Bring to a boil; reduce heat, and simmer, uncovered, 5 minutes, stirring occasionally.
13. Garnish servings evenly with reserved sliced greens.
14. Top with sour cream, if desired.
15. Serve with lemon wedges.

Dandelion Stew

Ingredients:

5 dried ancho chilies
4 garlic cloves, minced
1 bunch of dandelion greens (around 1/2 pound), discard stem ends and slice the greens
1 lb. red potatoes, sliced into 1/4" sized pieces
5 cups broth
Salt and pepper to taste
2 tbsps. fresh lemon juice
4 tbsps. extra virgin olive oil
grated parmigiano-reggiano cheese
Honey, optional

Directions:

1. Remove the ancho chili stems and seeds.
2. Slice or tear the chilies into 1 inch pieces.
3. Warm 2 Tbsps. of extra virgin olive oil in your soup pot, over medium heat.
4. Add the ancho chile peppers and minced garlic to the hot oil, stir until you smell the garlic.
5. Add the sliced dandelion greens with 1 tsp. of fine sea salt, and 1/4 tsp. black pepper, and stir.
6. Add the 5 cups of broth along with your potatoes, and turn the heat up to bring everything to a simmer. If you are using a parmigiano rind then add it now.
7. Let soup reach a simmer then salt to taste.
8. Allow the soup to simmer for 10 minutes to soften the potatoes.
9. Once potatoes are soft, turn off the heat and stir in 2 tbsps. of olive oil, 2 tbsps. of lemon juice, and add more salt if needed. now, if desired, stir in 2 tsps. of honey to balance the bitterness.
10. Serve the soup with fresh grated parmigiano-reggiano sprinkled on top.

Dandelion Potatoes

Ingredients:

5 lbs. white potatoes, peeled and cubed
3 tbsps. butter salt and pepper, to taste
1 pound bacon, diced
1 pound torn dandelion greens
1 medium onion, diced
1 egg, lightly beaten
1/2 cup white vinegar
1 tbsp. white sugar
1 tbsp. all-purpose flour

Directions:

1. Bring a large pot of salted water to a boil.
2. Add potatoes and cook until tender but still firm, about 15 minutes.
3. Drain, toss with butter, and season with salt and pepper.
4. Place bacon in a large, deep skillet.
5. Cook over medium high heat until evenly brown.
6. Remove the bacon and drain on paper towels. Set aside the pan with the bacon grease.
7. In a large bowl gently toss together the dandelion greens and onion.
8. In a small bowl, whisk together the egg, vinegar, and sugar.
9. Season with salt and pepper.
10. Stir the egg mixture into the skillet with the warm bacon grease.
11. Mix in the diced bacon and flour, and whisk for about 1 minute, until thickened to the consistency of salad dressing.
12. Pour at once over the dandelions and toss to coat.
13. Serve greens over the potatoes and enjoy!

Chinese Dandelion Dumplings

Ingredients:
2 pounds ground pork
2 cups minced dandelion greens
3 cups minced napa cabbage
1/2 cup minced bok choy leaves
4 green onions, white and light green parts only, minced
1 tbsp. minced fresh ginger root
3 cloves garlic, minced
1 (8 oz.) can bamboo shoots, drained and minced
3 tbsps. soy sauce
1 tsp. white pepper
1 tsp. kosher salt
1 tsp. white sugar
4 tsps. sesame oil
1 egg whites
1 tbsp. water
100 wonton wrappers
1/2 cup vegetable oil
2 tsps. chili oil, or to taste
3 tbsps. hoisin sauce
1/2 cup soy sauce
4 tsps. sesame oil
1 tsp. white sugar
3 tbsps. balsamic vinegar
1 tsp. minced fresh ginger root
2 tbsps. chopped green onion
2 cloves garlic, minced

Directions:
1. Mix pork, dandelion greens, napa cabbage, bok choy, 4 minced green onions, 1 tbsp. of ginger, 3 cloves of garlic, bamboo shoots, 3 tbsps. of soy sauce, white pepper, salt, 1 tsp. of sugar, and 4 tsps. of sesame oil.
2. Chill in the refrigerator 6 to 8 hours, or overnight.
3. Beat the egg white with the water in a small bowl and set aside.
4. Place 1 tbsp. of the pork mixture into a wonton wrapper, working one at at time.

5. Cover additional wrappers with a moist towel to prevent drying. Brush the edges of the wrapper with the egg white mixture.
6. Fold the wrapper and seal the edges with a moistened fork.
7. Spray a large skillet with cooking spray.
8. Heat 2 tbsps. for vegetable oil over medium-high heat.
9. Working in batches, place the dumplings into the skillet, seam side up.
10. Cook until the dumplings brown slightly, 30 seconds to 1 minute.
11. Pour 1/2 cup of water into the skillet and cover.
12. Gently steam the dumplings until the oil and water begin to sizzle, 7 to 8 minutes.
13. Once the water is cooked off, flip the dumplings and continue cooking until the bottom begin to brown, 3 to 5 minutes.
14. Repeat in batches with the remaining dumplings, oil, and water. Serve with dipping sauce.
15. To make dipping sauce: Combine chili oil, hoisin sauce, 1/2 cup of soy sauce, 4 tsps. of sesame oil, 1 tsp. of sugar, balsamic vinegar, 1 tsp. of ginger, 2 tbsps. of green onion, and 2 cloves of garlic in a bowl.

Dandelion Flower Cookies

Ingredients:

1/2 cup oil
1/2 cup honey
2 eggs
1 tsp. vanilla
1 cup unbleached flour
1 cup dry oatmeal
1/2 cup dandelion flowers

Directions:

1. Preheat oven to 375 degrees F.
2. Blend oil and honey and beat in the two eggs and vanilla.
3. Stir in flour, oatmeal and dandelion flowers.
4. Drop the batter by teaspoonfuls onto a lightly oiled cookie sheet and bake for 10-15 minutes.

Dandelion Greens and Tortellini Soup

Ingredients:

1 1/2 cups dry cheese tortellini
1 tbsp. butter
1 cup matchstick-sized carrots
1 onion, chopped
4 cups chicken broth
1 (15 oz.) can diced tomatoes, drained
2 cups chopped dandelion greens
1 tsp. garlic powder
1 tsp. dried basil
Salt and ground black pepper to taste

Directions:

1. Fill a large pot with lightly salted water and bring to a rolling boil.
2. Stir in tortellini and cook uncovered, stirring occasionally, until tender yet firm to the bite, 10 to 11 minutes.
3. Drain.
4. Melt butter in a large pot over medium heat.
5. Add carrots and onion; cook and stir until slightly softened, about 5 minutes.
6. Add chicken broth, tomatoes, dandelion greens, garlic powder, basil, salt, and black pepper.
7. Bring to a boil.
8. Reduce heat to medium-low and simmer until flavors combine, 10 to 15 minutes.
9. Serve and enjoy!

Sautéed Dandelion Greens

Ingredients:
1 lb. dandelion greens
2 cloves of garlic
3 tbsp. extra virgin olive oil
1 chili pepper
Salt to taste

Directions:
1. Pour the olive oil into a saucepan and place the pan over minimum flame.
2. Peel and crush the cloves of garlic, then cut the chili pepper in two half. If fresh chili is not available, use 1/2 tsp of chili flakes.
3. Cook the pepper and garlic very slow until ready to cook the dandelion greens.
4. Wash and raise the dandelion greens as times as need to eliminate any trace of dirt. Steam or boil the dandelion greens 5 minute.
5. If is possible, save the water used to steam or boil the vegetables.
6. Sauté the vegetables, until almost all the liquid is evaporated.
7. Add salt as needed a couple of minutes before ready.
8. Once cooked, the vegetables have to be juicy, but not washy.
9. Serve the sautéed dandelion greens hot or warm.

Dandelion Bread

Ingredients:

2 2/3 cups milk
2 eggs
3/4 cup honey
1/2 cup cooking oil
2 cups dandelion petals
1 tsp. salt
4 tsps. baking powder
4 cups flour

Directions:

1. Harvest dandelion petals.
2. Cut off the stem and the green parts and save only the petals.
3. Thoroughly wash your dandelion petals.
4. Preheat oven to 400 degrees F.
5. Grease 2 bread pans and set aside.
6. Combine dry ingredients, including dandelion petals.
7. In separate bowl mix all other ingredients well.
8. Then add to dry ingredients and mix thoroughly.
9. Harvest dandelion petals.
10. Cut off the stem and the green parts and save only the petals. Thoroughly wash your dandelion petals.
11. Preheat oven to 400 degrees.
12. Grease 2 bread pans and set aside.
13. Combine dry ingredients, including dandelion petals.
14. In separate bowl mix all other ingredients well.
15. Then add to dry ingredients and mix thoroughly.
16. Pour in bread pans and bake for 25 minutes or until knife inserted in center of bread comes out clean.

Tuna Salad with Dandelion

Ingredients:

2 (4.5 oz.) cans tuna in extra virgin olive oil, undrained
1/3 cup dandelion petals, loosely packed (about 3 flower heads)
1/4 cup freshly snipped chives
3-4 tbsps. sour cream
2 tsps. lemon juice
salt and pepper to taste

Directions:

1. Place all of the ingredients into a medium bowl, except salt and pepper. Blend together with a fork until combined.
2. Use more or less sour cream according to your family's preferences for texture.
3. Season to taste with salt and pepper.
4. Serve on bread, in lettuce wraps, or stuffed into other veggies and enjoy!

Sautéed Dandelions and Pine Nuts

Ingredients:

Large bunch dandelion greens, chopped
2 tbsps. olive oil
5 garlic cloves, sliced thin
1 tsp. crushed red pepper
1/2 cup vegetable broth
2 tbsps. pine nuts
Juice from 1/2 lemon
Salt and pepper to taste
1 splash of hot pepper vinegar sauce or apple cider vinegar

Directions:

1. Heat olive oil over medium heat until shimmering in a sauce pan.
2. Add the garlic and crushed red pepper.
3. Cook, stirring frequently just until the garlic starts to brown.
4. Add the chopped dandelion greens in and toss well to coat.

5. Pour in the vegetable broth and simmer, stirring occasionally over medium heat until the broth is almost completely absorbed.
6. Toss in pine nuts, lemon juice, then add the vinegar and mix to incorporate.
7. Serve and enjoy!

Dandelion Slaw

Ingredients:

1 bunch Dandelion greens, stems removed and leaves thinly sliced
1 large carrot, shredded
1/2 orange, juiced
1/2 lemon, juiced
Salt and ground black pepper to taste
1/2 red onion, very thinly sliced
1 slice cooked bacon, chopped
3 tbsps. mayonnaise
1 tbsp. olive oil

Directions:

1. Toss dandelion greens with carrot, orange juice, lemon juice, salt, and black pepper in a large salad bowl, using your hands to rub orange and lemon juice into dandelion leaves.
2. Let stand a few minutes to absorb flavors.
3. Fill a bowl with ice water.
4. Bring a saucepan of water to a boil and stir onion into boiling water.
5. Cook just until starting to soften, 15 to 30 seconds.
6. Drain and immediately immerse onion in ice water.
7. Drain ice water, blot onion dry on paper towels, and add to dandelions.
8. Stir bacon, mayonnaise, and olive oil into dandelion mixture and toss to coat.
9. Serve and enjoy!

Dandelion with Kiwi

Ingredients:

2 tsps. coconut oil
2 cloves garlic, chopped
1 tsp. minced fresh ginger
1/4 tsp. sea salt
1/2 tsp. freshly ground black pepper
2 kiwis, peeled and coarsely chopped
1 tbsp. fresh oregano leaves
1 bunch dandelion leaves, washed and sliced thin
2 tbsps. blanched slivered almonds

Directions:

1. Heat coconut oil in a skillet over medium-high heat.
2. Add garlic, ginger, sea salt and freshly ground black pepper; cook and stir until garlic begins to turn color, about 3 minutes.
3. Stir in chopped kiwi and oregano leaves and cook for another 2 minutes.
4. Add dandelion greens; lower heat to medium and cook until dandelion greens are dark green and tender, about 5 minutes.
5. Stir in slivered almonds and season to taste.
6. Serve and enjoy!

Mediterranean Dandelion Greens

Ingredients:

12 cups chopped dandelion greens
2 tbsps. lemon juice
1 tbsp. olive oil, or as needed
1 tbsp. minced garlic
1 tsp. soy sauce salt to taste
Ground black pepper to taste

Directions:

1. Place a steamer insert into a saucepan, and fill with water to just below the bottom of the steamer.
2. Cover, and bring the water to a boil over high heat.

3. Add the dandelion greens, recover, and steam until just tender, 7 to 10 minutes depending on thickness.
4. Whisk together the lemon juice, olive oil, garlic, soy sauce, salt, and black pepper in a large bowl.
5. Toss steamed dandelion greens into dressing until well coated.
6. Serve and enjoy!

Orzo with Dandelion Greens

Ingredients:

1 tsp. ground turmeric
2 cups uncooked orzo pasta
2 tbsps. olive oil
4 cloves garlic, sliced
1 bunch dandelion greens, stems removed and leaves coarsely chopped
1 large lemon, juiced
1/4 tsp. ground nutmeg
1/4 cup grated Parmesan cheese, or to taste
Salt and black pepper to taste

Directions:

1. Bring a large pot of lightly-salted water to a boil; sprinkle the turmeric over the boiling water and stir in the orzo; return to a boil.
2. Cook uncovered, stirring occasionally, until the pasta has cooked through, but is still firm to the bite, about 11 minutes; drain.
3. Scrape into a mixing bowl and set aside.
4. Heat the olive oil in a large skillet over medium heat.
5. Cook the garlic in the hot oil for a few seconds until it begins to bubble.
6. Stir the dandelion greens into the garlic, cover the skillet with a lid, and cook for 10 minutes.
7. Remove the cover and continue cooking and stirring until the dandelion greens are tender, about 10 minutes more.
8. Stir the dandelion mixture into the orzo along with the lemon juice, nutmeg, and Parmesan cheese.
9. Season with salt and pepper, serve and enjoy!

Dandelion Cheese Crisps

Ingredients:

2 bunches dandelion greens, washed and dried
2 cups shredded Cheddar cheese

Directions:

1. Preheat oven to 425 degrees F (220 degrees C).
2. Spray 2 baking sheets with cooking spray.
3. Remove the stems and ribs from the dandelion greens, and shred the greens very thinly.
4. Spread the shredded dandelion greens onto the baking sheets, and sprinkle evenly with Cheddar cheese.
5. Bake the dandelion greens for 10 minutes, watching carefully to prevent burning, until the dandelion greens are crisp and the cheese is browned.
6. Serve and enjoy!

Dandelion and Feta Salad

Ingredients:

1 bunch dandelion greens, finely chopped
1/2 tsp. salt
1 tbsp. apple cider vinegar
1 apple, diced
1/3 cup feta cheese
1/4 cup currants
1/4 cup toasted pine nuts

Directions:

1. Massage dandelion greens with salt in a large mixing bowl for 2 minutes.
2. Pour vinegar over the dandelion greens and toss to coat.
3. Fold apple, feta cheese, currants, and pine nuts into the dandelion greens.
4. Serve and enjoy!

Spinach and Dandelion Smoothie

Ingredients:

2 cups fresh spinach
1 cup almond milk
1 tbsp. peanut butter
1 tbsp. chia seeds (optional)
2 dandelion leaves
1 sliced frozen banana

Directions:

1. Blend spinach, almond milk, peanut butter, chia seeds, and dandelion leaves together in a blender until smooth.
2. Add banana and blend until smooth.
3. Serve and enjoy@

Tropical Dandelion Smoothie

Ingredients:

1 1/2 cups frozen pineapple chunks
1 cup chopped dandelion leaves
1 banana, cut in chunks
1 cup almond milk, or as needed

Directions:

1. Place pineapple, dandelion greens, and banana in a blender.
2. Add almond milk.
3. Blend until smooth.

Dandelion and Quinoa Salad

Ingredients:

1/2 cup water
1/4 cup quinoa
8 leaves dandelions, chopped, or more to taste
1/2 avocado, peeled, pitted, and cut into cubes
1/2 tomato, cut into cubes
1/4 cucumber, peeled and cut into cubes
1/4 cup crumbled feta cheese
2 tbsps. Italian-style salad dressing

Directions:

1. Bring water and quinoa to a boil in a saucepan.
2. Reduce heat to medium-low, cover, and simmer until quinoa is tender, 15 to 20 minutes.
3. Drain water and run quinoa under cold water to cool.
4. Place a steamer insert into a saucepan and fill with water to just below the bottom of the steamer.
5. Bring water to a boil.
6. Add dandelion greens, cover, and steam until tender, 2 to 3 minutes.
7. Place chopped dandelion greens in a bowl and refrigerate until chilled, 3 to 5 minutes.
8. Mix avocado, tomato, and cucumber together in a bowl.
9. Add quinoa and dandelion greens.
10. Sprinkle feta cheese over quinoa mixture.
11. Add Italian dressing and stir.

Waldorf Dandelion Salad

Ingredients:

1/2 cup walnuts, divided
4 cups chopped dandelion greens, or more to taste
1 cup thinly sliced celery
1 red apple, chopped and divided
6 tbsps. raisins, divided
2 tbsps. Dijon mustard
2 tbsps. water, or more as needed
1 tbsp. red wine vinegar
1/8 tsp. sea salt

Directions:

1. Heat a skillet over medium heat.
2. Toast walnuts in skillet until fragrant and lightly browned, 3 to 5 minutes.
3. Toss dandelion greens, celery, 1/2 of the apple, 1/4 cup walnuts, and 1/4 cup raisins together in a large bowl.
4. Combine remaining apple, walnuts, and raisins with Dijon mustard, water, red wine vinegar, and sea salt in a blender; blend until smooth, adding water as needed to thin the mixture so it blends completely.
5. Drizzle dressing over the salad and toss.

Dandelion Yam Wrap

Ingredients:

8 large dandelion greens, cut into small pieces
1/2 cup balsamic vinaigrette
2 tbsps. soy sauce
2 yams, quartered
1/2 (15 oz.) can black beans, rinsed and drained
1 1/2 tsps. olive oil
1/4 cup crumbled feta cheese
2 (9 inch) whole wheat tortillas, warmed

Directions:

1. Combine dandelion greens, balsamic vinaigrette, and soy sauce in a bowl.
2. Cover and marinate in the refrigerator for 1 hour.
3. Bring a large pot of water to a boil.
4. Add yam pieces and cook until soft when pierced with a fork, about 15 minutes.
5. Drain and cool; when yams can be handled, cut into cubes.
6. Warm black beans in a small saucepan over medium heat, 2 to 5 minutes.
7. Remove dandelion greens from vinaigrette mixture.
8. Cook and stir dandelion greens with olive oil in a skillet over medium heat until dark green, about 2 minutes.
9. Place half the yams on each tortilla and top yams with black beans, dandelion greens, and feta cheese.
10. Fold bottoms of tortillas partially over filling and roll to wrap the filling in the tortillas.

Creamy Parmesan Dandelion Chicken

Ingredients:

1 bunch dandelion greens, stemmed and chopped
1/2 cup water
2 tbsps. red wine vinegar
1 pinch sea salt
6 oz. skinless, boneless chicken breast, diced
3/4 cup heavy whipping cream
2 tbsps. butter
1/4 tsp. ground black pepper
1 (3 oz.) package grated Parmesan cheese

Directions:

1. Combine dandelion greens, water, red wine vinegar, and sea salt in a saucepan; cook over medium heat until the dandelion greens wilt, about 5 minutes.
2. Remove from heat and drain, reserving the liquid.
3. Set the dandelion greens aside.

4. Combine the reserved liquid and the chicken in the saucepan over medium heat.
5. Cook and stir until the chicken is no longer pink in the center, 7 to 10 minutes.
6. Stir the dandelion greens, cream, butter, and black pepper through the chicken; cook, stirring occasionally, until the butter melts and the mixture is hot, about 10 minutes.
7. Sprinkle Parmesan cheese over the mixture; cook and stir until the cheese melts and the sauce thickens, 3 to 5 minutes.

Dandelion Sweet Potato Bake

Ingredients:

2 tsps. olive oil
2 medium sweet potatoes, peeled and cubed
16 oz. Italian pork or chicken sausage links, cut into small rounds
2 cups finely chopped dandelion greens
3/4 cup milk
1/4 cup flour
2 cups chicken broth
3/4 cup shredded Gruyere cheese

Directions:

1. Heat the olive oil in a large pan over high heat.
2. Add the sweet potatoes and Italian sausage then stir to coat.
3. Cook for a few minutes until starting to brown and then move everything around.
4. Repeat until the sweet potatoes and sausage both have golden brown exteriors.
5. In a bowl, combine the sweet potato and sausage mixture with the dandelion greens.
6. Transfer to the lined baking dish.
7. Bring 1/2 cup milk to a low boil and then lower heat to simmer.
8. Whisk in the flour and remaining 1/4 cup milk to form a thick paste.
9. Add the broth, whisking to keep the sauce smooth.
10. Add 1/4 cup Gruyere and stir until melted.
11. Pour the sauce over the sweet potatoes, dandelion greens and sausage in the baking dish.

12. Top with remaining 1/2 cup cheese and bake for 10 minutes or until the sauce is bubbly and the cheese is melted.

Dandelion Root "Carrots"

You can cook dandelion roots and eat them like carrots.

Ingredients:

Dandelion roots

Directions:

1. Dig up dandelions in early spring using a spade.
2. Keep the taproot of each plant intact.
3. Pull the greenery from the plants. You can eat the leaves of the plants, either uncooked like salad greens or stewed separately from the roots in boiling water.
4. Rinse each dandelion root under cold water, removing all dirt. Check to make sure each root is free of insects.
5. Peel the outer skin from each taproot using a paring knife. The skin is bitter tasting.
6. Cover the roots with water in a pan, and bring them to a boil on the stove.
7. Reduce the heat and simmer the roots.
8. Test doneness by stabbing one or two roots with a fork.
9. When the fork easily goes into the taproots, they are ready.
10. Drain the water from the dandelion roots, rinse them with warm water and serve.
11. Season the roots as you would carrots.

Red Potato and Sautéed Greens Salad

Ingredients:

1 lb. baby red potatoes
1 large bunch of dandelion greens
1 head of chicory
3 tbsp. extra virgin olive oil
2 garlic cloves, minced
1 can white kidney beans, rinsed

Zest and juice of a lemon
2 tbsp. ricotta
Salt and pepper to taste

Directions:

1. Boil potatoes until tender. Drain and slice in half. Set aside.
2. While potatoes boil, trim ends of dandelion greens and chicory.
3. Rinse well (but do not dry) and cut into large pieces. Heat oil in a large skillet and add garlic, stirring just until golden.
4. Add the greens and sauté just until wilted, about 3 minutes.
5. Season with salt and pepper.
6. Add the white kidney beans and boiled potatoes to the skillet.
7. Toss contents together and then add lemon zest, juice and ricotta.
8. Toss contents again to evenly coat.
9. Salt and pepper to taste.

Spicy Sautéed Dandelion Greens and Onions

Ingredients:

4 lbs. dandelion greens, tough (lower) parts of stems discarded and leaves cut crosswise into 2-inch pieces
2 tbsps. extra-virgin olive oil, plus additional for drizzling
2 tbsps. unsalted butter
2 large onions, halved and thinly sliced
4 large garlic cloves, coarsely chopped
1/2 tsp. crushed red pepper
Salt and freshly ground black pepper

Directions:

1. Cook greens in salted boiling water, uncovered, until ribs are tender, about 10 minutes per batch.
2. Scoop out into a colander, then rinse under cold water to stop cooking.
3. Drain well, gently pressing out excess water, and transfer to a bowl.

4. Heat oil and butter in cleaned pot over medium heat until foam subsides, then cook onions with garlic, crushed red pepper, 1/2 tsp. salt, and 1/4 tsp. pepper, covered, stirring occasionally, until pale golden, about 8 minutes.
5. Add greens and cook, covered, stirring occasionally, until onions are tender, 4 to 6 minutes.
6. Drizzle with additional oil and serve!

Dandelion Greens with Eggs

Ingredients:

4 cups dandelion greens, chopped thick stems removed
2 tbsps. unsalted butter, clarified butter, or ghee
1 large leek, white and light green parts only, finely chopped
4 large eggs
1/4 cup crumbled feta cheese

Directions:

1. Bring a large pot of salted water to a boil.
2. Add the chopped dandelion greens and blanch for 1 to 2 minutes.
3. Drain the greens thoroughly, using a wooden spoon to drain and press out as much liquid as possible.
4. Melt the butter or ghee in a 10-inch sauté pan set over medium heat. Sauté the leeks until tender, about 5 minutes, stirring occasionally.
5. Add the drained dandelion greens one handful at a time.
6. Cook each handful until wilted, then add more.
7. When the greens are wilted, crack the eggs into the pan on top of the greens. Top with feta cheese and cook uncovered until the whites of the eggs are set, about 5 minutes.

Pasta with Sausage and Dandelion Greens

Ingredients:

1 lb. pasta
Olive oil

1/4 lb. Italian or spicy sausage, crumbled
4 cloves garlic, minced
Four big handfuls of dandelion greens
1/2 cup grated Pamesan cheese

Directions:

1. Cook the pasta in salted water. It should cook for just 12-13 minutes.
2. Drain and set aside.
3. In the same big pot you cooked the pasta in, heat a little olive oil and add the crumbled sausage and garlic.
4. Cook over medium heat until the sausage is cooked through.
5. Add the greens and cook until barely wilted, then add the pasta and cheese and stir until all is combined and gooey - about two minutes. Serve with extra cheese.

Dandelion Fritters

Ingredients:

4 cup dandelion flowers snapped off at the top of stem
1 cup biscuit mix
1 cup milk
1 tbsp. sugar or honey (optional)
1/2 inch oil in skillet

Directions:

1. Mix together the biscuit mix and milk. Dip dandelion flowers in mix one at a time and douse well with batter.
2. Heat oil in skillet to 335 degrees F. or until it sizzles when a bit of batter is dropped into it.
3. Drop flowers into hot oil head first. Fry until golden brown on both sides.
4. Remove and drain. Serve hot or cold.

Dandelion Salad with Honey Dressing

Ingredients:

6 cup dandelion greens
6 oz. bacon
2 tbsp. red wine vinegar
2 tsp. honey
2 tsp. dijon mustard

Directions:

1. Pull stems from the dandelion leaves. Wash greens well and put in a bowl.
2. Cut bacon into 1 inch pieces. Fry bacon until brown and drain on paper towels. Reserve 1/4 cup bacon fat.
3. Combine vinegar, honey, and mustard.
4. Add to pan and cook over low heat for 1 or 2 minutes, scraping up any brown bits stuck to the bottom of the pan.
5. Add reserved fat and stir until hot.
6. Pour over greens immediately; toss and serve.

Breaded Dandelion Blossoms

Ingredients:

1/4 cup milk
2 tbsp. powdered milk
1 tbsp. baking powder
1 egg
1/2 cup flour
Pinch of salt
16 lg. fresh dandelion blossoms
Vegetable oil for frying

Directions:

1. Mix all ingredients except dandelion blossoms and fat. Wash blossoms lightly; drain. Do not allow to wilt. Dip blossoms into batter.
2. Heat oil in a pan.
3. Fry until golden.
4. Serve and enjoy!

Wilted Bacon Dandelions

Ingredients:

5 strips bacon, cut into 1 inch pieces
1/4 cup vinegar
1/3 cup sugar
Salt to taste
Young dandelions, cut into 1 inch pieces
2 onions, cut up

Directions:

1. Fry bacon until crisp.
2. Add vinegar, sugar and salt.
3. Combine dandelions and onions.
4. Pour bacon mixture over dandelions, wilt.

Scalloped Dandelions

Ingredients:

2 tbsp. bacon drippings
2 tbsp. flour
3/4 cup water
2 cup milk
3/4 tsp. salt
1 tbsp. vinegar
2 tsp. sugar
1 cup dandelion greens
1/4 cup minced onion
2 hard boiled eggs, sliced

Directions:

1. Combine the drippings and flour in a skillet and cook, stirring, until lightly brown.
2. Add the water, milk, salt, vinegar and sugar. Chop dandelion greens and mix with onion.
3. Add the sauce, but do not cook after adding.
4. Add eggs last. Do not use dandelions with flowers. 6 servings.

Dandelion and Lime Iced Tea

Ingredients:

8 cups dandelion flowers, rinsed
12 cups cold water
1 cup hot water
Juice of 3-4 limes
2-3 tbsp. sweetener (your choice)

Directions:

1. Mix sweetener and warm water.
2. Add lime juice then add cool water.
3. Stir well then add the dandelion flowers.
4. Mix well
5. Refrigerate for at least 3-4 hours.
6. Drain out the flowers.
7. Serve and enjoy!

Pennsylvania Dutch Dandelion Salad

Ingredients:

Dandelion greens
4 thick slices bacon, cut in small pieces
1/4 cup butter
1/2 cup cream
2 eggs, beaten
1 tsp. salt
Black pepper
Paprika
1 tbsp. sugar
1/4 cup cider vinegar

Directions:

1. Carefully wash and prepare dandelion greens as you would lettuce.
2. Never use dandelion greens after they have begun to flower, because they are apt to be bitter.
3. Roll in cloth and pat dry. Put green into a salad bowl and set in a warm place.
4. Fry bacon and turn out onto greens. Put the butter and cream into skillet and warm over low heat.
5. Mix into the beaten eggs the salt, pepper, paprika, sugar and vinegar; blend into slightly warm cream mixture. Increase heat and cook, stirring constantly until mixture thickens.
6. Pour hot dressing over greens; toss gently and serve at once.

Italian Sausage and Dandelions

Ingredients:

Brown 2 pounds of bulk sausage.
Add water and a little tomato sauce (optional).
Cook for 1 hour. Boil dandelions separate until tender.
Mix the 2 together and let come to a boil.

Directions:

1. In a bowl beat 5 eggs and a handful of Romano cheese.
2. Add it to the boiling mixture and continue to cook, stirring until the egg is cooked and coated on the dandelions.

Pan-Fried Beans and Dandelion Greens

Ingredients:

8 oz. (1/2 bunch) dandelion greens
1 onion, thinly sliced
2 cloves garlic, minced
12 oz. (2 cups or one 15-oz. can) cannelloni or other white beans, drained and rinsed
Zest from one lemon
Juice from 1/2 lemon
1 tsp. za'atar spice blend
1 to 2 tsps. salt
Good-quality extra-virgin olive oil

Directions:

1. Trim the center stem from the dandelion greens and slice the leaves cross-wise into ribbons. Chop the stems into bite-sized pieces.
2. Heat one tsp. of oil in a large skillet over medium-high heat.
3. Cook the onions with 1/2 tsp. salt until they are very soft and uniformly golden-brown, 8 to 10 minutes.
4. Stir in the garlic and the chopped dandelion stems, 1 minute. Transfer the onion mixture to a bowl.

5. Warm another 1 to 2 tsps. of oil, enough to coat the entire bottom of the pan.
6. Add the beans and spread them into a single layer.
7. Cook for 2 minutes without stirring.
8. Stir and spread them out again.
9. Repeat until all the beans are blistered all over. Adjust the heat as needed to prevent burning the beans.
10. Stir the dandelion leaves, the za'atar, and another 1/2 tsp. of salt into the beans.
11. Stir until the dandelion greens are completely wilted and tastes tender, 3 to 5 minutes.
12. Add the onion mixture back in, along with the lemon zest and juice from 1/2 lemon.
13. Stir and taste.
14. Add more lemon juice, salt, or other seasonings to taste.
15. Serve immediately, drizzling a little extra-virgin olive oil over each dish.
16. Add a poached egg, a scoop of pasta, or a piece of toast to make a more complete meal. The beans will lose their crispiness as they cool, but leftovers still make a tasty meal. This dish will keep refrigerated for up to a week.

Lemon and Garlic Sautéed Dandelions

Ingredients:

Washed dandelion
Olive oil
Minced garlic
Salt
Lemon
Parmesan cheese
Red pepper
Capers
Onion, chopped

Directions:

1. Heat olive oil, and a bit of garlic, in a non-stick skillet.
2. Once the garlic has become flavorful, add dandelion greens.

3. Cook on medium-high until wilted, 3-5 minutes.
4. Sprinkle with salt, spritz with lemon juice.
5. Add Parmesan cheese, red pepper, capers, chopped onion and serve.

Dandelion Vinegar

Ingredients:

Fresh dandelion greens
Apple cider vinegar, at room temperature
1 glass mason jar
Herbs such as fresh thyme, oregano, rosemary or dill

Directions:

1. Coarsely chop the herbs then fill a glass jar to the top with the herbs.
2. Pour room-temperature apple cider vinegar over the herbs until it is full to the top.
3. Cover jar with a plastic screw-on lid. Don't use metal lids because they react to the vinegar in a nasty way
4. If you use unpasteurized vinegar a film will form called, 'the mother'.
5. Simply skim it off when you decant.
6. Label your vinegar with the date and the type of herbs you used.
7. Place jar in a dark place like a kitchen cupboard or pantry shelf for 6 - 8 weeks.
8. Strain out the herbs and bottle your vinegar. No metal lids.

Brown Rice and Dandelion Salad

Ingredients:

4 cups vegetable broth
2 cups brown rice
3 tbsps. butter
1/2 cup diced onion
1/2 cup diced celery
1/2 cup diced carrot
1/4 cup chopped almonds

1/2 cup diced mushrooms
Salt to taste
2 cups chopped dandelion greens

Directions:

1. Bring broth and brown rice to a boil in a saucepan.
2. Reduce heat to medium-low, cover, and simmer until rice is tender and liquid has been absorbed, 45 to 50 minutes.
3. Melt butter in a large saucepan over medium heat; cook and stir onion, celery, carrot, and almonds until onion begins to softened, 5 to 10 minutes.
4. Add mushrooms and cook 1 minute more; season with salt.
5. Mix cooked rice into onion mixture until evenly combined.
6. Add dandelion greens and cook until completely wilted, about 5 minutes.

Boiled Dandelion Greens

Ingredients:

Dandelion greens
Butter
Lemon
Salt and pepper to taste

Directions:

1. Bring a pot of water to a boil.
2. Add the dandelion leaves.
3. Boil for two minutes.
4. Drain the water.
5. Fill the pot with water again and bring to a boil.
6. Add the dandelion leaves again.
7. Boil greens for 2 more minutes.
8. Drain.
9. Add butter, salt, pepper and lemon.
10. Serve and enjoy!

Dandelion Greens Salad

Ingredients:

Dandelion greens
Finely chopped red onion
Fresh basil
Grape tomatoes
Goat cheese
Pears
Walnuts
Apples
Hardboiled eggs

Directions:

1. I always use a basic olive oil and red wine vinegar dressing on my salads (which is cheap and low in calories).
2. Remember, dandelion greens are best eaten raw before they produce a yellow flower.

Cauliflower Dandelion Soup

Ingredients:

1 tbsp. extra-virgin olive oil
4 cups chopped cauliflower (about 1 medium head)
2 med. shallots, chopped (or 3 if small)
4 garlic cloves, finely chopped
5 cups chicken or vegetable broth
2 heaping cups chopped or torn dandelion greens (no thick stems)
1/2 medium ripe avocado, pitted and diced
Sea salt and black pepper, to taste

Directions:

1. Heat the olive oil in the bottom of a soup pot or Dutch oven.
2. Add the cauliflower and shallots.
3. Cook, stirring occasionally, for 5-7 minutes until the shallots are soft.
4. Add the garlic.
5. Stir for 1 minute.
6. Add the broth.

7. Bring to a boil, then reduce heat to medium-low, cover, and simmer for 10-15 minutes or until the cauliflower is just tender.
8. Remove from heat and stir in the dandelion greens until wilted. Allow the soup to stand, uncovered, for 10 minutes.
9. Stir the avocado into the soup. Use a blender to puree the soup until it is thick and creamy.
10. Serve and enjoy!

Dandelion Burgers

Ingredients:

1 cup packed dandelion petals (no greens)
1 cup flour
1 egg
1/4 cup milk
1/2 cup chopped onions
1/4 tsp salt
1/2 tsp garlic powder
1/4 tsp each basil and oregano
1/8 tsp pepper

Directions:

1. Mix all ingredients together.
2. Form into patties and pan fry in oil or butter, turning until crisp on both sides.

Korean Cauliflower Dandelion Pancakes

Ingredients:

1 cup Chopped Cauliflower
1/2 Cup Chopped Dandelion Greens
1/2 Cup Chopped Scallions
1/4 Cup Rice Vinegar
1/2 Tbsp. Gochujang
1/2 Tbsp. Korean Chile Flake
1/2 Cup Flour

1/4 Cup Water More or less

Directions:
1. Mix the cauliflower, dandelion, scallion, vinegar, gochujang, and chile flake in a bowl with a pinch of salt and let marinade for a half hour, stirring occasionally.
2. Make a dipping sauce with some sesame oil, chile flake, scallions, and soy sauce.
3. Mix the flour into the cauliflower mixture, then add the water as needed to form a thick batter.
4. Fry in a frying pan on high heat for about 4 minutes a side to brown and cook through.
5. Serve with the dipping sauce.

Dandelion Moonshine

Ingredients:

2 gallons of water
4 quarts of dandelion blossoms
4 lbs. of sugar
2 packets of bread yeast
6 oranges
5 lemons

Directions:
1. Wash dandelions and pour them into large pot
2. Make sure you get only the flowers remove all stems and leaves.
3. Pour 2 gallons of boiling water over them and let stand for 24 hours
4. Strain through cheese cloth and pour into Carboy
5. Add grated rind and 6 oranges, 5 lemons and 4 lbs. sugar to dandelion wine
6. Make A Yeast Starter using 2 tsps. of yeast and add it to the Carboy.
7. Keep temperature between 18 C -23 C until fermentation is complete.
8. Distill once fermentation is complete
9. Add a tiny bit of honey and toasted American oak chips to the to the hearts and bottle in 500ml mason jars

10. Let Dandelion moonshine age for 1- 3 months before drinking

Dandelion Flower Tea

Ingredients:

8 dandelion flowers
12 oz. boiling water
Honey

Directions:

1. Pour boiling water over flowers
2. Let steep for 5 minutes
3. Add honey
4. Serve and enjoy!

Dandelion and Lemon Biscuits

Ingredients:

Approx 20 flower heads
1/2 cup butter
1 cup caster sugar
1 egg
Zest of 1 lemon, plus 1 tbsp. juice
1 1/2 all-purpose flour
1/4 cup corn flour
1/4 tsp baking powder
Pinch of salt

Directions:

1. Wash, then remove the yellow petals by pinching firmly and pulling.
2. Cream the sugar and butter until fluffy.
3. Add the egg and lemon zest.
4. Sift in the dry ingredients and combine well.
5. Add in the lemon juice and petals and mix.
6. Dollop spoonfuls onto a baking tray and cook for approximately 12 mins at 350 degrees F until golden.
7. Cool on a wire rack and enjoy!

Dandelion Flower Pasta

Ingredients:

10.6 oz. semolina flour
1/2 tsp. salt
0.7 oz dandelion flowers
2 Tbsp oil
1/2 cup water

Directions:

1. In a bowl, combine the semolina flour with the salt.
2. In a high speed blender, combine the dandelion flowers, oil and water, and blend until smooth and no pieces remain.
3. Pour into the semolina flour, and mix until a dough forms.
4. Knead the dough for 5 minutes, allow it to rest for 5 minutes, then knead it further for 5 minutes.
5. Wrap the dough in plastic or cover with a damp towel, and allow it to rest at least 30 minutes. It can be refrigerated for a day or so if tightly wrapped.
6. Cut the dough ball into quarters, and use a pasta roller to roll it out into flat sheets, starting at level 1 and rolling it down to level 5 thickness, re-folding and rolling it again if it is falling apart. The more you work it, the smoother it becomes.
7. Dry the pasta and store, or cook in plenty of salted, boiling water, about 2-3 minutes, until al dente.
8. Toss with butter or a sauce, and serve.

Dandelion Mead

Ingredients:
8 cups of dandelion flowers
1 cup of lemon balm tops
1/2 cup of strawberry leaves
Zest and juice of 2 lemons
1 cup of raisins
1/3rd package of champagne yeast
4 cups plus one tsp. of local honey
Equipment:
2 (1 gallon) glass jugs
1 funnel
1 strainer
1 wine siphon and tube
1 fermentation lock with drilled rubber stopper that fits the top of the glass jug (size #6)
4 to 5 spring lock wine bottles 750 ml each or normal wine bottles with corks
Wine corker (if using corks)
8 quart stock pot
Metal strainer or sieve

Directions:
1. Gather the dandelion flowers while they are open.
2. Wash flowers, lemon balm tops, and strawberry leaves and run them through a salad spinner to remove as much water as possible.
3. Cut up the leaves and use dandelion flowers whole.
4. In a stock pot, bring 1 1/2 gallons of water to a boil.
5. Once it is boiling rapidly put the flowers and leaves in the pot. Shut off the heat.
6. Add the raisins, lemon zest and juice.
7. Don't add the honey or the yeast yet.
8. Cover the pot and let the mixture steep until the temperature drops to about 110 degrees F. Strain the plant material to get all the liquid out. Discard the plant material.
9. Reserve the liquid. Take 1 cup of the liquor and add 1 tsp. of honey. Stir to dissolve the honey.

10. Sprinkle 1/3rd of a package of champagne yeast over the top of the liquor in the cup measure.
11. Set it aside until the yeast bubbles up.
12. Meanwhile, clean and sanitize one of the glass jugs, the stopper and fermentation lock, and the funnel.
13. Everything that comes in contact with the wine should be cleaned and sanitized before use, to insure a good ferment.
14. Into the remaining liquor, stir in the remaining 4 cups of honey, until completely dissolved.
15. When the liquor is cooled to 100 degrees F, and the wine yeast is bubbly and active, stir the wine yeast into the liquor.
16. Pour into one of the glass jugs.
17. Cap with a fermentation lock and set aside to ferment.
18. After four weeks, once the fermentation has slowed down, siphon the mead from the first jug into the second jug, leaving any dregs in the first jug.
19. The dregs are the scum that is left over at the bottom of the jug.
20. Wash the jug and put it away till later. This will clean the dregs out of the jug. Sanitize the fermentation lock and put it on the second jug that is now holding your mead.
21. Set the jug aside.
22. This should activate the fermentation again and allow the mead to clear. After three to four more weeks, the fermentation will slow down.
23. Check by gently shaking the jug with the mead.
24. If the mead foams up and forms a head of foam on top of your mead, wait two more weeks and check again.
25. The actual time will vary depending on your ambient temperature.
26. When the fermentation stops, transfer the mead to the first jug once again.
27. Remember to sanitize this jug before you transfer the mead to it. At this point I usually cap the jug with a twist cap rather than the fermentation lock.
28. If you were making regular wine instead of mead, this is the point that you would bottle your wine.
29. However, mead is a little different.
30. Sometimes it will appear that the fermentation has stopped only to start up again a week later.

31. So at this point I check for signs of fermentation by untwisting the twist cap every 24 to 48 hours.
32. If you hear a hiss, indicating that there is pressure inside the jug, let the pressure off and check again in a day or two.
33. After there are no indications of pressure build up inside the jug, wait at least 10 more days checking every day or two.
34. After this, it is safe to bottle your mead.
35. When you are ready to bottle, siphon mead from the jug into each wine bottle.
36. Leave any dregs in the wine jug.
37. Complete the caps or corks. Label and date your dandelion mead.
38. Set aside for at least six months before drinking.
39. Dandelion mead will be good in December, with a strong honey flavor.
40. It will be even better the following May.

Dandelion Greens Sauté

Ingredients:

1-2 med. onions, sliced finely or chopped
2 tbsp. olive oil
1 tsp. toasted sesame oil
2 tsp. sesame seeds
1 large bunch of fresh dandelion leaves

Directions:

1. Sauté onions and garlic in olive oil.
2. Trim the leaves and prepare the greens by rinsing in a colander
3. Add wilted greens to the pan of onions and garlic.
4. Toss with toasted sesame oil.
5. Sprinkle with sesame seeds
6. Serve and enjoy!

Dandelion Frittata

Ingredients:

4 eggs
1/2 cup grated parmesan, feta, or cheddar cheese
2 tbsps. plain yogurt
1 bunch of fresh nettle leaves, stems removed and chiffonade cut
1 to 2 handfuls of fresh dandelion flowers, washed and dried
1/2 onions, thinly sliced
2 cloves garlic, crushed
2 sun-dried tomatoes, chopped
1 tbsp. capers
Salt and pepper to taste

Directions:

1. Preheat oven to 400 degrees F.
2. In a cast iron skillet, sauté onions in olive oil over medium heat until caramelized.
3. Add garlic and cook for another minute.
4. Add the nettle leaves and dandelion flowers and sauté for another minute or two.
5. In a mixing bowl, whisk together eggs, yogurt, and cheese.
6. Add chopped sun-dried tomatoes, capers, and season with salt and pepper.
7. Spread veggie mixture evenly on bottom of the skillet.
8. Pour egg mixture into the skillet and gently stir together until the veggies are covered, then allow to cook for a few minutes.
9. When the egg mixture is about half set, put the whole pan in the oven.
10. Bake for 7-10 minutes, until puffy and golden around the edges.
11. Remove the pan from the oven and let stand for several minutes.
12. Serve and garnish each plate with a dandelion flower.

Mushroom Garlic Dandelion Quiche

Ingredients:

3 1/2 cups dandelion greens
1/2 lb. mushrooms
9 eggs
1/2 cup grated Romano cheese
1 tbsp. olive oil
1-2 cloves garlic, minced
2 tbsp. parsley, fresh, minced
Sea salt and black pepper to your taste
1 dash hot pepper flakes
1 Pie shell, (optional)

Directions:

1. If you are making 'with crust, partially bake the pie shell at 450 degrees for 5-7 minutes or until lightly browned.
2. Remove from the oven and set aside.
3. Reduce oven to 325 degrees F.
4. For a crust-less version; preheat the oven to 325 degrees
5. Cook 3.5-4 cups of dandelion greens in salted boiling water until wilted but not completely cooked.
6. Drain using a colander.
7. Chop the dandelion greens into bite-sized pieces.
8. Sauté the minced garlic in the olive oil and add the mushrooms and green onions.
9. After about 5 minutes, add the dandelion greens.
10. The mixture is ready when all the liquid has cooked off.
11. Beat 9 eggs in a bowl.
12. Season with salt and pepper and dash of hot pepper flakes
13. Add the cheese and stir.
14. Put the greens mixture into the pie shell or directly into a pie or quiche pan.
15. Pour the egg mixture over the greens.
16. Bake at 325 degrees for about 35 minutes or until the eggs are set.

Dandelion Tart

Ingredients:

1 bunch dandelion greens, about 12 oz.
 Salt to taste
2 tbsps. extra virgin olive oil
1 small onion, chopped
1 cup sliced mushrooms
1 or 2 garlic cloves, minced
4 large or extra large eggs
3/4 cup low-fat milk
Freshly ground pepper to taste
3/4 cup Gruyère cheese, grated
1 yeasted olive oil crust

Directions:

1. Bring a large pot of water to a boil, and fill a bowl with ice water.
2. When the water comes to a boil, salt generously and add the dandelion greens. Blanch four minutes and transfer to the ice water.
3. Drain, squeeze out excess water and chop.
4. Preheat the oven to 375 degrees.
5. Heat the olive oil in a large nonstick skillet over medium heat, and add the onion.
6. Cook, stirring, until tender, about five minutes, and add a pinch of salt and the mushrooms.
7. Cook, stirring, for four to five minutes, until the mushrooms have softened and the onions are golden.
8. Add the garlic and cook for another minute, then stir in the dandelion greens.
9. Stir together for a minute, and remove from the heat.
10. Season to taste with salt and pepper.
11. Beat the eggs in a large bowl. Brush the bottom of the pastry shell, and place in the preheated oven for five minutes.
12. Remove from the oven. Whisk the milk into the eggs, add 1/2 tsp. salt, freshly ground pepper to taste and stir in the cooked vegetables and cheese. Turn into the crust.
13. Bake 35 to 40 minutes, until set and the top is lightly browned.

Dandelion Leek Frittata

Ingredients:

4 tbsps. olive oil
1 large leek
2 tsps. each salt and black pepper
1 bunch fresh dandelion greens
6 eggs
1 tsp. each cumin and coriander powder
Juice from 1/2 a lemon
2 tbsps. stone ground mustard

Directions:

1. Chop the large leek into rounds. Heat the olive oil in a skillet and add the leeks.
2. Reduce the heat to medium-low.
3. Add the salt and black pepper, cover, and simmer for 5 minutes.
4. Add the dandelion greens. Simmer until most of the liquid has cooked out of the vegetables, about 10 minutes more.
5. Preheat the oven to 375 degrees F.
6. Grease a pie plate with olive oil.
7. In a bowl, beat the 6 eggs, cumin, coriander, and a splash (about 4 tbsps. each) of water and lemon juice.
8. Pour the egg mixture over the top of the greens and bake for 40 minutes.

Dandelion Lemon Cupcakes

Dandelion Cupcakes Ingredients:

1-2 cups dandelion petals
1 1/2 cups blanched almond flour
3 eggs
1/3 cup honey
2 tbsps. goat milk butter melted (or oil of your choice)
Zest from 1 lemon
1 tsp. lemon juice
1/2 tsp. baking soda
1 tsp. vanilla extract
1 pinch of sea salt

Buttercream Frosting Ingredients

1/3 cup goat milk butter softened
1/3 cup palm shortening pro-forest certified
1/4 cup raw honey or powdered sweetener
1 tsp. vanilla
Zest from 1 lemon

Directions:

1. Separate out the yellow dandelion petals from the green bitter stems.
2. Pinch the green base of each flower and gently pull the yellow petals free.
3. Discard the green base.
4. Process the dandelion petals soon after harvesting for best results.
5. Preheat oven to 325 degrees F.
6. Set dandelion petals aside to add in last, and then mix ingredients together in order that they are listed, starting with almond flour.
7. Lastly, fold in dandelion petals.
8. Spoon batter into 10 to 12 muffin cups lined with muffin liners.
9. Bake for 18 to 22 minutes.
10. Cupcakes are done when a toothpick poked inside of one comes out clean.
11. Mix buttercream frosting ingredients together in a mixing bowl using a hand blender or immersion blender.

12. Frost cupcakes after they have fully cooled.
13. Serve and enjoy!

Dandelion Sun Dried Tomato Bake

Ingredients:

1 bunch dandelion greens (washed, dried and chopped)
1 onion (chopped small)
2 garlic cloves (minced)
1/4 cup sundried tomatoes
1 tsp. dried red pepper flakes
2 eggs
1 1/4 cup heavy cream
1 cup Gruyere cheese (grated or chopped fine)
3 cups day-old bread (cubed) (if using fresh, cube and toast)
Salt and pepper to taste

Directions:

1. In a large skillet, heat a drizzle of olive oil and add the onions, garlic, red pepper flakes, and sundried tomatoes.
2. Cook on medium until soft (about 5-8 mins).
3. Add the Dandelion greens, salt and pepper, stir and heat until wilted.
4. Then hold to the side off the heat.
5. Preheat oven to 350 degrees F.
6. In a large bowl, whisk together the eggs, cream and shredded cheese, then add the bread cubes to soak.
7. Add the Dandelion mixture into the bowl with the cream and bread, fold to incorporate.
8. Pour the contents into a 13x9inch baking dish.
9. Bake for about 45 mins to 1 hour or until set.
10. Allow some of the bread cubes to stick out the top for a crunchy, crispy topping.
11. Cut into squares and serve.

Dandelion Root Zucchini Cake

Ingredients:

1 1/2 cup white flour
1 cup whole wheat flour
1/2 cup dandelion root powder (or cocoa powder)
1 1/2 tsp baking powder
1 tsp baking soda
1 tsp cinnamon
3/4 tsp salt
3 eggs
1 1/4 cup sugar
1/2 cup apple sauce
1/3 cup canola oil
2 tsp vanilla
2 cups packed, grated zucchini
1/2 cup chocolate chips (optional)

Directions:

1. Preheat oven to 350 degrees F.
2. Grease 2 8x4 inch loaf pans.
3. In a large bowl, combine flour, cocoa, baking powder, baking soda, cinnamon, salt
4. In a medium bowl, whisk eggs, sugar, applesauce, oil, vanilla.
5. Stir in zucchini to wet mixture.
6. Add wet ingredients to dry ingredients.
7. Stir just until moistened.
8. Add chocolate chips.
9. Pour into pans.
10. Bake for 50 minutes.
11. Cool in pans for 5 minutes then cool on wire rack.
12. Yield: 2 loaves

Rhubarb Dandelion Pie

Ingredients:
3 cups rhubarb chopped into bite sized pieces
1/2 cup dandelion flowers
2 eggs
1 1/2 cups unrefined or cane sugar
1 1/2 tsp vanilla extract
3 tbsps. flour
Crumb topping:
3/4 cup flour
1/2 cup brown sugar
1/3 cup butter softened at room temperature
1 unbaked 9" pie crust

Directions:
1. Heat the oven to 400 degrees F.
2. Chop the rhubarb stalks into bite size pieces and place them in a mixing bowl.
3. Cut the flower petals from the green base and stem.
4. A tiny bit of green with the petals is okay but too much will make it bitter.
5. Mix the dandelion flower petals in with the rhubarb.
6. Beat the eggs.
7. Stir in the vanilla, sugar and flour.
8. Pour over the rhubarb and dandelion mixture and stir.
9. Pour the filling into the pie crust.
10. With a fork or pastry blender, mash the butter, flour and brown sugar to create a crumbly mixture.
11. Sprinkle this mixture onto the top of the pie.
12. Bake for 10 minutes then reduce the heat to 350 degrees and bake for another 35-40 minutes.
13. When done, the crust will be a golden brown and the rhubarb will be soft when stuck with a fork.
14. Remove from the oven and let it sit for a few minutes to cool.
15. Serve and enjoy!

Dandelion Root Bitters

Ingredients:
1/2 cup dried dandelion root
4-5 ribbons orange zest
1 inch piece ginger, sliced
1 750ml bottle vodka

Directions:
1. Put the dried herbs into a quart sized jar, then pour in the entire bottle of vodka.
2. Cover the jar and let sit for 4-6 weeks.
3. It will turn orange from the zest, and the dandelion root will expand.
4. Strain out the herbs with a fine mesh sieve, and your dandelion root bitters are finished!

Dandelion Squash Salad with Quinoa

Salad Ingredients:
3 cups quinoa, cooked
3 cups favorite winter squash, cooked
2 cups dandelion greens, rinsed, trimmed, chopped
1/2 cup red onion, diced
Parsley, for garnish
1 tbsp. olive oil
1 garlic clove, minced
Salt and pepper to taste

Vinaigrette Ingredients:
1/4 cup olive oil
2 tbsps. whole grain mustard
1 tsp. red wine vinegar
1 squeeze lemon juice
Salt and pepper to taste

Salad Directions:

1. In a medium skillet preheated to medium heat, add olive oil, garlic, and dandelion greens with salt and pepper.
2. Cook until softened and remove from heat.
3. To serve the salad, combine quinoa and squash. Top with dandelion greens, red onion, and parsley. Drizzle vinaigrette over the top!
4. In a bowl, whisk all the vinaigrette ingredients together until combined.
5. Serve and enjoy!

Blueberry Dandelion Green Smoothie

Ingredients:

1 tbsp. raw cacao powder
1 tbsp. hemp powder or seeds
3/4 cup coconut water
1/3 cup frozen blueberries
1/2 cup dandelion greens
1/4 avocado

Directions:

1. Mix all ingredients in a blender.
2. Puree until smooth.
3. Serve and enjoy!

Dandelion Peanut Butter Cookies

Ingredients:

1/2 cup butter, softened
1/2 cup peanut butter
1/2 cup Honey
1 egg
1 tsp. vanilla extract
1 tsp. baking soda
1 cup all-purpose flour
1 cup whole wheat flour
1/2 cup Dandelion Petals (just the petals)

Directions:

1. Preheat oven to 400 degrees.
2. Line cookie sheets with parchment paper or silicone baking mats.
3. Sift together the flours and baking soda. Set aside.
4. Cream together the butter, peanut butter, and honey until light and fluffy. Beat in the egg and vanilla extract until thoroughly incorporated.
5. Add the sifted dry ingredients to the butter mixture and mix until a soft dough forms.
6. Fold in the dandelion petals.
7. Drop by Tbsps. full onto prepared baking sheet.
8. Bake in preheated oven for 13 to 15 minutes or until edges are golden.
9. Cool on wire racks.

Dandelion Honey

Ingredients:

3 cups dandelion petals
4 cups water
3 lemon slices
1/2 vanilla bean (split in half)
2 1/2 cups granulated sugar

Directions:

1. Pick dandelion flowers during the daylight while in full bloom.
2. Soak the flowers in cold water for five minutes to allow time for any insects to exit.
3. Remove the petals, then measure the petals only. Discard the center of the flower and the stem.
4. Place the petals in a heavy saucepan along with the water, lemon slices, and vanilla bean.
5. Bring it to a boil, reduce the heat, and simmer it for 30 minutes.
6. Remove the pan from the heat and let steep for 6 hours.
7. Strain the dandelion tea through a cheesecloth and discard the solids.
8. Place the dandelion tea in a heavy saucepan and bring it to a low boil.
9. Gradually add sugar to the boiling liquid while stirring until the sugar is dissolved.
10. Lower the heat and let it simmer uncovered until it reaches the desired syrupy thickness. This may take up to 4 hours.
11. Store dandelion honey in the refrigerator.

Dandelion Petal Sorbet

Ingredients:

1 quart dandelion blossoms
3 cups water
1/2 cup sugar
1/2 cup mild honey
3 tbsps. lemon juice

Directions:

1. As soon as possible after picking the blossoms, use a pair of sharp scissors to snip the yellow portions of the petals from the green calyxes, leaving the bitter white bottoms of the petals still attached to the calyxes. Discard the calyxes.
2. Heat the water, sugar, and honey in a small saucepan.
3. As soon as the syrup comes to a boil, remove it from the heat and stir in the yellow petals.
4. Cover and let steep for at least one hour then strain the syrup through a fine sieve.
5. Stir in the lemon juice and chill.
6. Freeze the mixture in an ice cream maker according to manufacturer's directions.

Dandelion Flower Schnapps

This schnapps has a fresh, aromatic and sweet acid taste. The color is yellow, dark yellow or reddish golden.

Ingredients:

Dandelion flowers
Clear, unflavored vodka - 40% alcohol content (80 proof)

Directions:

1. Pick the flowers in spring or early summer, just before they open or right after.
2. Clean flowers thoroughly.
3. Remove the green sepals with a small, sharp knife as they are very bitter.
4. Use a clean glass jar with tight-fitting lid.

5. Fill 2/3 of the jar with flower heads.
6. Cover with vodka.
7. Leave some air above.
8. Let steep in a dark place at room temperature, 64-68 degrees F (18-20 degrees C)
9. Steep for 1-7 days.
10. Shake lightly and taste it from time to time.
11. Strain and filter your infusion into a clean glass bottle or jar with tight-fitting lid.
12. The flower schnapps should be enjoyed within a couple of days.
13. Storage (aging) doesn't improve the flavors. On the contrary.

Dandelion Root Schnapps

Dandelion root schnapps will be dry, spicy and very aromatic with a pleasant bitter taste.

Ingredients:

Dandelion roots
Clear, unflavored vodka - 40% alcohol content (80 proof)

Directions:

1. Use fresh dandelion roots.
2. Dig the roots from late autumn till early spring. That's when they are most aromatic.
3. Direction:
4. Clean roots thoroughly.
5. Roots: Let the roots dry for a couple of days in the shade on a paper towel.
6. Slice roots thinly.
7. Use a clean glass jar with tight-fitting lid.
8. Fill 2/3 of the jar with sliced roots.
9. Cover with clear, unflavored vodka - 40% alcohol content (80 proof).
10. Leave some air above.
11. Let steep in a dark place at room temperature, 18-20°C (64-68 degrees F).
12. Steep for 1-7 days.
13. Shake lightly and taste it from time to time.

14. Strain and filter your infusion into a clean glass bottle or jar with tight-fitting lid.
15. The root schnapps can be very muddy. It might be necessary to filter it a couple of times.
16. This schnapps can be stored for several months in a dark place at room temperature.

Dandelion Petal Risotto

Ingredients:

1 tbsp. extra-virgin olive oil
1 tbsp. butter
6 cups vegetable or chicken broth
1 spring onion, diced
1 cup risotto rice
1/2 cup white wine
1 bunch dandelion greens, washed and coarsely chopped
1/2 cup grated aged Asiago cheese

Directions:

1. Combine the oil and butter in a heavy, large skillet over medium-high heat.
2. Warm the stock in a saucepan, covered to keep it from evaporating.
3. Add the chopped white bulb of the onion and cook until soft and translucent, about 2-3 minutes.
4. Stir in the rice to coat with the oil, and cook for 1 minute.
5. Add the white wine and stir, cooking until absorbed by rice.
6. Begin to add the broth, 1/2 cup at a time, stirring after each addition and waiting until the broth is absorbed by the rice before adding the next 1/2 cup.
7. After 10 minutes of cooking, stir in the chopped dandelion leaves.
8. When the rice is al dente, turn off the heat.
9. Add the last 1/4 cup of broth and the grated cheese.
10. Season with salt and pepper, garnish with the sliced green onion stems and any dandelion petals.
11. Serve and enjoy!

Dandelion Lip Balm

Ingredients:

3 tbsps. dry dandelion flowers
3 of coconut oil or olive oil
1 tbsp. beeswax

Directions:

1. Gently melt the oil in a double boiler.
2. Add the dandelion.
3. Cover.
4. Stir the dandelion into the oil well.
5. Allow the oil to simmer gently for 20-30 minutes.
6. Turn off the heat and keep the pot covered.
7. Allow the dandelions to sit in the oil for another hour and even overnight.
8. The dandelions will continue to infuse into the oil as it sits.
9. Separate the dandelion solids from the oil using a mesh strainer.
10. This may require re-heating to oil if it has infused over night, but you will need to re-heat it anyway.
11. Using your dandelion-infused oil, reheat the oil and add the beeswax and stir.
12. Have your lip balm tubes ready.
13. As soon as the oil and beeswax have warmed and integrated, fill your lip balm tubes or salve containers.
14. Allow to sit until cool.

Dandelion Jam

Ingredients:

2 cups Dandelion flowers, green bit removed
2 cups boiling water
Zest of 1 lemon
Juice of 1 lemon
3 cups sugar and pectin mix (check pectin packaging for measures)

Directions:
1. Place two cups of dandelion heads into a mixing bowl and add the zest of one lemon.
2. Pour two cups of boiling water over top.
3. Leave overnight to infuse.
4. The next day, pour the mixture through a sieve to separate all the leaves.
5. Add lemon juice and bring to a boil.
6. Add the sugar and pectin and boil rapidly for 10 minutes, then take a side plate, and using a spoon, drop a couple of drops onto the plate.
7. If the drops are runny, boil for another few minutes and keep testing until the drops on the plate are set.
8. Skim of the top layer of 'scum' that develops, then pour the mixture into warm jars.
9. Remove the air bubbles with a wooden spoon or similar.
10. Add the lids and screw tops and put aside in a cool place for 24 hours.
11. The heat will cause the lid to 'suck in' so the jam will be air tight.

Dandelion Curried Red Lentil Soup

Ingredients:

1 large onion, chopped
2 cloves garlic, minced
1 sm. jalapeño, seeds removed and diced
1 tsp. ginger paste
1 tsp. whole cumin
1 tsp. ground turmeric
1/2 tsp. coriander
1/2 tsp. ground cumin
1/8 tsp. red chilli pepper or cayenne pepper
1 1/2 cups red lentils, rinsed
5 1/2 cups water
Salt, to taste
4 cups chopped dandelion greens

Directions:

1. Simmer the soup in a large pot for about 35 to 45 minutes or until lentils are cooked.
2. Add the salt, check the seasoning, and add more if necessary.
3. Add additional water if the soup is too thick.
4. Add the dandelion greens and simmer on low heat for about 10 minutes, or until the greens are tender.
5. Serve and enjoy!

Dandelion Tacos

Ingredients:

1 1/2 tbsps. olive oil
1 large onion, cut into 1/4-inch slices
3 cloves garlic, minced
1 tbsp. red pepper flakes, or to taste
1/2 cup chicken broth
1 bunch dandelion greens, chopped
1 pinch salt
12 corn tortillas
1 cup crumbled queso fresco cheese
3/4 cup salsa

Directions:

1. Heat the olive oil in a skillet over medium heat.
2. Stir in the onion; cook and stir until the onion has softened and turned golden brown, about 10 minutes.
3. Add the garlic and red pepper flakes, stirring until fragrant, about 1 minute.
4. Stir in the chicken broth, dandelion greens, and salt.
5. Cover and reduce heat to low. Simmer until the greens are nearly tender, about 5 minutes.
6. Remove lid and increase heat to medium, stirring until the liquid evaporates, about 5 minutes.
7. Remove from heat and set aside.
8. Heat another skillet over medium-high heat.
9. Warm the tortillas in the skillet for about 1 minute per side. Fill the warmed tortillas with the dandelion greens.
10. Top with the queso fresco cheese and salsa.

Dandelion Zucchini Muffins

Ingredients:

Cooking spray
3 tbsps. butter
5 slices bacon, diced
3/4 cup diced onion
1 tsp. minced garlic
8 dandelion leaves, stems removed and leaves thinly sliced
2 cups shredded zucchini
3 eggs
1 tsp. salt
Freshly ground black pepper to taste
1 cup all-purpose flour
1 tsp. baking powder
3/4 cup finely shredded Swiss cheese

Directions:

1. Preheat oven to 400 degrees F (200 degrees C).
2. Generously spray 12 muffin cups with cooking spray.
3. Melt butter in a skillet over medium heat; add bacon.
4. Cook gently until bacon begins to curl, 3 to 5 minutes.
5. Add onion, garlic, and dandelion leaves.
6. Cook and stir until dandelion greens have wilted, stirring occasionally, 5 to 8 minutes.
7. Transfer greens mixture to a large bowl.
8. Stir in zucchini, eggs, salt, and black pepper.
9. Add flour and baking powder; mix until flour is evenly distributed and moistened.
10. Stir in Swiss cheese.
11. Spoon batter into prepared muffin tin.
12. Bake in the preheated oven until edges of muffin turn golden brown, about 20 minutes.
13. Serve and enjoy!

Tuscan Dandelion and Cannellini Bean Soup

Ingredients:

2 slices smoked bacon, finely chopped
1 onion, chopped
1 clove garlic, minced
1/4 tsp. freshly grated nutmeg
1/8 tsp. crushed red pepper flakes
6 cups chicken broth, or more as needed
1 (15 oz.) can cannellini beans, drained and rinsed
2 tbsps. chopped sun-dried tomatoes
2 oz. Parmesan cheese rind
1 bunch dandelion greens
1/4 cup uncooked small pasta, such as orzo
5 large fresh sage leaves, minced
5 leaves fresh basil, coarsely chopped
1 tbsp. grated Parmesan cheese, divided
1 tbsp. extra-virgin olive oil, divided

Directions:

1. In a large saucepan over medium heat, cook the bacon, onion, garlic, nutmeg, and red pepper flakes until the onion is translucent, about 5 minutes.
2. Pour in chicken broth and cannellini beans, and bring the mixture to a boil.
3. Stir in sun-dried tomatoes and the Parmesan cheese rind.
4. Reduce heat to a simmer, and cook while you prepare the greens, about 10 minutes.
5. Cut the stems from the dandelion leaves, and slice the stems into pieces about 3/4-inch long.
6. Cut the dandelion leaves into 1-inch wide ribbons.
7. Stir the dandelion stems and pasta into the soup, setting aside the leaves.
8. Reduce heat to a simmer, and gently simmer until the pasta is tender, about 10 minutes.
9. Stir the dandelion leaves, sage, and basil into the soup, and simmer just until wilted, 3 to 4 minutes.
10. Serve with Parmesan cheese and a drizzle of olive oil.

Dandelion Pasta

Ingredients:

1/3 pound spaghetti
2 tbsps. extra-virgin olive oil
1 clove garlic, minced
1 bunch dandelion greens, chopped
1 tsp. capers salt and pepper to taste
1 tsp. lemon juice, or to taste
1/4 cup grated Parmesan cheese

Directions:

1. Fill a large pot with lightly salted water and bring to a rolling boil over high heat. Once the water is boiling, stir in the spaghetti, and return to a boil.
2. Cook the pasta uncovered, stirring occasionally, until the pasta has cooked through, but is still firm to the bite, about 8 minutes.
3. Drain well in a colander set in the sink.
4. Meanwhile, heat the olive oil in a large skillet over medium heat.
5. Stir in the garlic, and cook for 1 minute to soften.
6. Add the dandelion leaves.
7. Cook and stir until the stems of the dandelion grees are tender. You can use some of the hot pasta water to help steam the dandelion greens in the covered pan.
8. Stir the hot spaghetti into the dandelion greens mixture along with the capers.
9. Season to taste with salt and black pepper, and drizzle with lemon juice.
10. Sprinkle with Parmesan cheese to serve.

Dandelion Cabbage Soup

Ingredients:

1/2 head cabbage, chopped
4 dandelion leaves, torn into several pieces
3 leaves kale, torn into several pieces

4 green onions, chopped
1/2 cup chopped red bell pepper
1/2 cup thin carrot slices
1/2 cup chopped celery
3 cubes chicken bouillon
3/4 cup chopped bacon
1 tsp. dried marjoram
1 tbsp. dried parsley
1 tsp. dried sage water, to cover

Directions:

1. Process cabbage, dandelion greens, kale, green onions, bell pepper, carrot, and celery in a food processor until finely chopped.
2. Transfer to a slow cooker.
3. Add chicken bouillon, bacon, marjoram, parsley, and sage.
4. Pour enough water over the ingredients to fill slow cooker to the brim of the crock.
5. Slow cook on medium 2-3 hours.
6. Serve and enjoy!

Stuffed Dandelion Leaves

Ingredients:

16 lg. dandelion leaves
2 1/2 cup cooked brown rice
1 onion, chopped
1/4 cup oil
1 1/2 cup cottage cheese
1 egg, beaten
1/2 cup chopped parsley
3/4 cup raisins
1 tsp. dill weed
3/4 tsp. salt

Directions:

1. Preheat oven to 350 degree.
2. Sauté onion in oil.
3. Mix all ingredients except dandelion leaves.
4. Remove stems.

5. Place 2 tbsps. of filling on the underside of the leaf and roll up into a square packet.
6. Place seam side down in a greased casserole.
7. Cover and bake for about 30 minutes or steam in steamer basket over boiling water until the leaves are tender, about 20 minutes.
8. Bake any extra filling and serve with stuffed leaves.

Dandelion Cannelloni

Ingredients:

12 cups roughly chopped dandelion leaves
12 to 16 cannelloni shells
2 tbsp. olive oil
3/4 cup diced onion
2 cloves garlic, minced
2 cup sliced mushrooms
1/4 cup minced fresh parsley
1 1/2 cup sm. curd cottage cheese
1 1/2 cup Parmesan cheese
1 tbsp. lemon juice
3 to 4 cups spaghetti sauce

Directions:

1. Heat oven to 350 degrees F.
2. Steam dandelion greens 3 to 5 minutes and drain.
3. When cooled, wring out excess water.
4. Cook shells until barely tender.
5. Drain, set aside.
6. Heat oil, sauté onion and garlic for 2 minutes.
7. Add mushrooms and parsley, sauté until tender.
8. In large bowl, combine dandelion greens, sautéed vegetables, cottage cheese, 1 cup of grated Parmesan cheese and lemon juice.
9. Season with salt and pepper. Stuff shells, place some of sauce in bottom of 9 inch pan and line with stuffed shells.
10. Cover with remaining sauce and Parmesan cheese.
11. Bake 30 to 40 minutes then serve!

Dandelion Bisque

Ingredients:

1 bunch (about 1 lb.) dandelion greens
1 (14 oz.) can chicken broth
1/4 cup butter
1 cup chopped mushrooms
3 tbsp. flour
1/4 tsp. curry powder
1 pt. half and half
Salt & pepper
4 slices bacon, crisply fried & crumbled

Directions:

1. Wash dandelion greens well; drain.
2. Cut off and thinly slice the white stems.
3. Slice the leaves separately.
4. Place stems in a frying pan, add 2 tsps. of the broth, cover and cook over medium heat until tender, about 4 minutes.
5. Add the leaves and 1 more tsp. of the broth if needed, and cook, covered until limp, about 3 minutes longer.
6. Turn dandelion greens and remaining broth into a blender and whirl until smooth.
7. In a frying pan, melt butter over medium heat; add mushrooms and sauté 5 minutes.
8. Stir in flour and curry powder; cook until bubbly. Slowly add the cream.
9. Cook, stirring until thickened.
10. Add dandelion greens puree and salt and pepper to taste.
11. Garnish with the crumbled bacon.
12. Serve and enjoy!

Dandelion Almond Loaf

Ingredients:

1/2 lb. dandelion greens
1 med. onion, chopped
1 clove garlic, minced
1/4 cup oil
2 cup ground almonds or walnuts
1 cup whole grain dried bread crumbs
1/2 cup wheat germ
1 egg, beaten
2 tbsp. chopped parsley
1 tsp. oregano
1/2 tsp. cumin
1/2 cup catsup
1 tsp. tamari soy sauce

Directions:

1. Preheat oven to 350 degrees F.
2. Wash, chop and steam greens for 5 minutes using a tsp. of water.
3. Sauté onion and garlic in oil. Grind almonds in blender.
4. Combine almonds, crumbs, wheat germ, eggs, greens, sautéed onions and garlic.
5. Add remaining ingredients.
6. Mix well. Pack into well-oiled 9x5x3 inch loaf pan.
7. Bake in preheated oven for 30 minutes.

Raisin and Pine Nuts Dandelion Fettuccine

Ingredients:

1/2 cup gold raisins
1 bunch dandelion greens
6 tbsp. unsalted butter
4 garlic cloves, minced
1 bunch spinach, trimmed
1 1/2 tsp. fresh lemon juice
1 lb. fettuccine
1 cup (4 oz.) grated Parmesan cheese
1/2 cup toasted pine nuts
1 tbsp. minced fresh chive
2 tbsp. minced fresh thyme
2 tbsp. minced fresh marjoram or 3/4 tsp. dried, crumbled
Salt and pepper

Directions:

1. Place raisins in small bowl.
2. Add enough hot water to cover. Let stand until plump (10 minutes).
3. Drain.
4. Remove stems and ribs from dandelion greens. Thinly slice enough greens to measure 1/2 cup.
5. Slice dandelion leaves into 1/2 inch wide strips.
6. Melt butter in heavy large skillet over medium heat.
7. Continue cooking butter until golden brown, stirring constantly (7 minutes).
8. Add minced garlic and sliced dandelion leaves.
9. Cook until dandelion greens are tender and wilted, stirring frequently (3 minutes).
10. Add greens and stir until wilted (2 minutes).
11. Stir in raisins and lemon juice.
12. Meanwhile, bring large pot of salted water to boil.
13. Add fettuccine and add 1/2 cup dandelion greens to boiling water and cook until pasta is just tender but still firm to bite.
14. Drain pasta and greens. Transfer to large bowl.

15. Add greens mixture, 1 cup grated Parmesan cheese, pine nuts and herbs.
16. Toss thoroughly.
17. Season pasta with salt and pepper.
18. Serve and enjoy!

Dandelion Patties

Ingredients:

1/2 cup cooked dandelion greens, chopped
1 cup bread crumbs
1/4 cup Parmesan cheese
1 egg, slightly beaten
Salt and pepper to taste
1 cup olive or cooking oil

Directions:

1. Drain chopped cooked dandelion greens well.
2. Mix thoroughly with crumbs and cheese.
3. Add egg and seasonings.
4. Shape into 3-inch patties about 1/2-inch thick.
5. Fry in hot oil until golden brown on both sides.
6. Serve and enjoy!

Dandelion Minestrone Soup

Ingredients:

1/4 lb. dried white nave beans
4 tbsp. olive oil
1 lg. onion
2 stalks celery
1 slice raw ham, diced
1 sm. cabbage
2 carrots
8 large dandelion leaves
1/2 cup corn (frozen okay)
1/2 cup green beans
1 sm. (10 oz.) can chopped tomatoes, strained
2 qts. stock (beef and chicken)
5 tbsp. chopped parsley
2 tbsp. chopped basil
1 tsp. ground rosemary
1/4 tsp. ground clove
Sm. dash of chili powder or cayenne
1/2 cup Parmesan cheese, grated
1/2 lb. pasta

Directions:

1. Soak beans in warm water for 12 hours. Then drain.
2. Pour half the oil into a soup pan and sauté over low heat the onion, celery and ham.
3. Add the cabbage, carrots, dandelion greens and the beans and tomatoes.
4. Pour the stock into the pan.
5. Add the ground clove and rosemary.
6. Bring to a boil and then simmer for about 45 minutes.
7. Meanwhile, place the remaining oil, the garlic, parsley, basil, cheese and the chili pepper into a blender and reduce to a pulp.
8. To the vegetable soup, add the corn, green beans, pasta and pulp mixture, and cook until pasta is done. Salt and pepper to taste.
9. Sprinkle with Parmesan cheese.
10. Serve and enjoy!

About the Author

Laura Sommers is **The Recipe Lady!**

She is the #1 Best Selling Author of over 80 recipe books.

She is a loving wife and mother who lives on a small farm in Baltimore County, Maryland and has a passion for all things domestic especially when it comes to saving money. She has a profitable eBay business and is a couponing addict. Follow her tips and tricks to learn how to make delicious meals on a budget, save money or to learn the latest life hack!

Visit her Amazon Author Page to see her latest books:

amazon.com/author/laurasommers

Visit the Recipe Lady's blog for even more great recipes:

http://the-recipe-lady.blogspot.com/

Laura Sommers is also an Extreme Couponer and Penny Hauler! If you would like to find out how to get things for **FREE** with coupons or how to get things for only a **PENNY**, then visit her couponing blog **Penny Items and Freebies**

http://penny-items-and-freebies.blogspot.com/

Other Cookbooks by Laura Sommers

- Recipes For The Lumbersexual
- Recipes for the Zombie Apocalypse: Cooking Meals with Shelf Stable Foods
- Recipes for the Zombie Apocalypse, Vol. 2: Cooking With Foraged Foods
- Egg Recipes for People With Backyard Chickens
- Super Awesome Casserole Recipes: The Ultimate Cookbook for the One Dish Meal

May all of your meals be a banquet
with good friends and good food.

Made in the USA
Las Vegas, NV
13 March 2022